# The System Redesigned— This Time for Children

## (and Taxpayers)

Norma Simpson

Couralad Management Corporation
Carson City, Nevada

THE SYSTEM REDESIGNED

FIRST EDITION
Copyright © 1998 by
Norma Simpson



ISBN 0-7880-1417-X                                          PRINTED IN U.S.A.

*Dedicated with love to*

*Courtney, Alex, Adam, Claire, Elaine, and Grace*

# Acknowledgments

My deepest appreciation goes to many people without whom this book could not have been written.

To my husband, Ron, I am grateful for so many things, your love, support, wisdom, encouragement, and for your certainty that I could do this when I was fairly certain I could not. Nothing I've done could have been done without you.

To Martha H. Phillips, a superb editor and dear friend, I am grateful for your incomparable gift—the time and effort to edit this work—so generously given. I thank you also for your belief in the book out of your love and compassion for children.

To Alma Stewart, my friend, and fellow teacher,  your shared experiences as an elementary teacher were invaluable.  I thank you also for the countless hours graciously given and for your willingness to undertake any task whatsoever to see this book published for the children's sake.

My appreciation goes to the physicians who spoke with me.  I especially thank Dr. Robert Gregory, Pediatrician, Medical School Clinical Professor, and Dr. Beatrice C. Lampkin, Professor Emerita of Pediatrics, University of Cincinnati College of Medicine, Cincinnati Children's Hospital Medical Center, for their expert medical advice and information.

I thank Dr. Jeanne Chall, Professor of education, Emeritus, Harvard University, for her time and effort on my behalf.  I also thank everyone who granted me an interview or shared their personal experiences with me.  You truly are the backbone of the book.

I also thank Deborah, Ken, David, Patti, Linda, Herb, Shannon, Roxanne, Amy, Margie, Wayne, Tom, Betty, Bill, Jean, Sam (wherever you are), and my mother Ann Spaulding for their love, support, and contributions to this book and to my life.

# Preface

This book includes many of my own experiences as a teacher. These experiences involve different school districts, different grade levels, and different states. The book also includes the experiences of teachers, parents, administrators, and board members from across the country.

To my surprise, wherever I interviewed people the dilemmas were the same, regardless of area. My intent was never to pinpoint any one school system, any one state, or any one person. (If you find yourself in this book, therefore, you are one among many.) Rather, my intent has been to put you, my readers, in the actual situations our children face so that you feel what they feel under those circumstances.

I ask you to read this book from the heart and then join me in redesigning the system — this time for the children.

Norma Simpson

Norma Simpson is available as a speaker on issues regarding children and the educational system.  She can be contacted at:

Norma Simpson
P.O. Box 58385
Cincinnati, Ohio 45258
(513) 922-1917

# TABLE OF CONTENTS

# Introduction

First time at school, a young child tries,
Too soon an eager spirit dies,
Must not we all most fierce despise
What dims the light in children's eyes?

Nevertheless that light has been dimmed, and it grows dimmer day by day as puzzled leaders, taxpayers, and parents search for answers that continue to elude them. While they search, our children's performance levels continue to fall and many of our best teachers leave the profession.

Unfortunately, those searching for answers have been able to identify only bits and pieces of the problems because they have been looking at our schools from the outside in, which keeps the picture obscure and fragmented. Everyone must begin looking at the inside from the inside. The only way to do this is to allow a primary elementary teacher to provide you with an "in-the-trenches" perspective. This approach will take you inside a working elementary classroom where—through a teacher's eyes—you will see why so many of our children struggle unnecessarily and to no avail.

They struggle because the system has forgotten certain things regarding how our children develop and learn. As a teacher, I have watched the aftereffect of what has been forgotten about children. I have watched the eagerness die within their eyes and have seen the hurt that replaced it. I have watched them give up within "the system." That is one of the reasons I have written this book. Another is to show taxpayers the vast amount of waste their ever-increasing tax dollars are supporting.

It is time to look, not at where our problems become evident, but to where they begin. It is time to apply the irrefutable law that we cannot change any situation until we find the source of the problem and attack it at its root. This is so universal a truism that it's a puzzling phenomenon that it has not occurred to us to work on education from that perspective. Instead, we have repeatedly tried to make the corrections at the top with quick-fix tax levies and patchwork philosophies, and have ignored the foundation. It is time to look at how a child learns. We have been looking at how to maintain a system.

Many people have asked me the following: "So, you have an answer for our schools; what is it?" However our current educational situation amounts to a series of problems that call for more than "an answer." It is now time to bring these problems together (all in one book) so we can look at them and then determine a course of action that is attainable, affordable, and educationally correct.

This I have done.  In the end, we shall see that our educational dilemmas are not a hopeless myriad of difficult, expensive, and unsolvable problems.  Fixing the system would be simple.  The difficult part is changing current attitudes regarding education that keep us focused on what adults want rather than on what children need.

Teachers are impotent regarding change.  Because they  can merely report, the only hope our country has for remaining a world leader is left to you, the public.  It is you who must bring about a genuine reformation of our school system.  This book explains how.

It is predicated on the principle that change can be right or good or effective only when, in the hands of the right people, it comes from full knowledge—only when it comes from the whole truth.  You, the public, have never had that.

Writer and columnist Sydney J. Harris once said,

> "Originality does not consist in saying something new—any madman can do that—but in expressing an old thought in such a way that it can never again be viewed in its former dimensions."[1]

This book takes you inside a teacher's workplace to show you what is happening to the children in our schools and to reveal where we must begin if we are to address our current failure to educate them properly.  It is my hope that after this experience you will never again be able to view our children or our schools in their former dimensions.

*      *      *

Can the system be redesigned correctly? Absolutely, although there are those who think not.  One acquaintance recently said, "It'll be a snowy day in hell before anything changes in this system."

13

She epitomizes the despair and hopelessness within us all—parents, teachers, and taxpayers alike.  So, if you want to be informed, put on your snowshoes and walk with me through the hell of our present-day educational systems.

We can call them "hell" can't we?  I mean, isn't hell any place or thing at all that dims the light in children's eyes?

# Chapter 1

THE SYSTEM:  When Teachers Aren't Allowed to
Teach in the Ways Children Learn


We'll remember long
and treasure,
That which has been learned through laughter—
and with pleasure.


An old fable tells of a group of animals who decided to start a school for their children.  So they hired some educators to design a program and to write a curriculum for them.

Running, flying, perpendicular tree climbing, and burrowing were the subjects, and everyone had to take all the courses (and at the same pace) so they would be well-rounded learners and graduate at the same time.

And so school began. The little rabbit started off well making straight A's in running, but he soon found himself making failing grades in flying. When the system insisted that he keep trying, he fell off a branch and broke his leg. Then his grades began to fall in running as well.

The bird was great in flying, but failed running and burrowing. She broke her wing during one relay race and her beak during a burrowing exercise. The squirrel and gopher were "below average" students because some of their grades brought down some of their other grades. And the owl? Well, he failed running, burrowing, climbing, and flying. Because he had to drop out of school altogether, his real talents were never recognized or developed.

Such things happen within our educational system as well because those who design the system take neither teacher nor child into consideration. Instead, both are handed impossible tasks and time schedules. One of the teacher's impossible tasks is forcing children to do impossible tasks.


## The Prerequisites of Education

The result of our current approach is that teachers see the children losing, missing out, and not learning because adults have forgotten the two inalienable prerequisites of education—individual need and readiness. This concept of individuality considers the uniqueness of each child and then teaches to that uniqueness in an environment where he or she can be successful. The concept of readiness requires that a child be physically and mentally ready for a task before being expected to perform it, regardless of age.

These were the first concepts I was taught in becoming a teacher and the last concepts I was able to apply after I began teaching. They were the first taught because they are fundamental to understanding how children—or any of us—learn. They were the last applied because "the system" takes precedence over education. Preoccupied with its own survival and expansion, the system has grown increasingly top-heavy and overburdened with officials, administrators, and "experts."

Teachers have watched the shifting emphasis become almost entirely riveted on the system and how to maintain it, even if it meant forsaking individual need and readiness in the process— which we did. And as the importance of the system grew, the importance of the children lessened.

Now our system, like a huge hot-air balloon, keeps deflating and descending in spite of the billions of dollars we pour into it each year. Our frenzied efforts are focused on keeping aloft all the unnecessary administrative positions the public has been convinced are needed until we can pass yet one more tax levy, and then another. In the process, we have trampled our children underfoot and demanded the impossible of our teachers.

For example, in one district, as more administrators were hired, ways had to be found to pay the additional salaries. One way involved putting more and more children  into each classroom. Where a State limit didn't exist, as many as 35 to 40 children were placed in a classroom. Later, when the State limited class size to 30 children, each classroom had 30 children, but the larger the class, the smaller the chance of meeting the needs of the children.

In another district, as enrollment dropped, one classroom after another was divided up to provide offices for more and more administrative personnel. Unfortunately, the teachers were the only ones asking, "If you have fewer and fewer children, why do you need more and more administrators?" In many districts, taxpayers are still waiting for an answer to that question.


## <u>"Mainstreaming" Versus Individual Need and Readiness</u>

In this book I do not use the term "mainstreaming" in its narrowest sense (i.e., the inclusion of handicapped children in the regular classroom). I believe that all children, regardless of physical disabilities, should be placed along the same guidelines. Rather, throughout this book, the term mainstreaming is used in its broadest sense (i.e., the throwing together in the classroom of all children, regardless of their states of readiness, their mental capabilities, or the speed with which they can move ahead).

In this type mainstreaming, after kindergarten, children are put into large classes and forced to fit into one of two pigeonholes— normalcy or retardation (regardless of their needs). Some systems include a third category—the gifted program. This category, however, is usually the last to be added and the first to be cut.

Surely everyone knows by now that the intelligence and ability levels of the children of our country are many and diverse. Perhaps not as well understood is the fact that their learning styles and their paces of learning are also varied and diverse. Yet the system forces teachers to teach from the false premise that every child can begin to learn at the same chronological age in large classes, can reach the same level of achievement and mastery of the written word as every other child, and can do it at the same pace. But children cannot learn under any premise that ignores individual need and readiness.

Instead of looking at our children realistically and providing for their differences or developing each child to be all that he or she can be, mainstreaming lumps them all together, feeds them all the same information, and expects them all to come out as carbon copies of each other in 12 years' time, with the same education and the same knowledge. Those who are unable to keep up are simply discarded along the way. As in the case of the owl, then, their special talents, bents, gifts, and abilities are never discovered; and many are thrown into society unprepared for anything other than unemployment, welfare, or crime.

For 17 years, I watched struggling children and those needing special help become lost in the shuffle and glow of the brighter students. I also saw the brighter students grow bored and lose interest when the needs of the slower children set the pace. Involuntarily, teachers had to make a choice. It was impossible to plan programs that would satisfy the many different needs and learning styles required for each child to work at his or her optimum level—not to mention State requirements, paperwork, time restrictions, and demands of supervisors. Something had to give; and without exception, it was the educational well-being of the children.

Consider the enigma that teachers face. They are keenly aware of our country's need for superior learners to solve our many and varied technological, environmental, and sociological problems. They are also aware of the need for brilliant qualified leaders. Yet they find themselves receiving watered-down materials and textbooks designed to dip down and bring the "unready" children along.

Mainstreaming hurts. It hurts the gifted, who are held back until they lose interest and motivation. It hurts the slower children, who are forced to move ahead faster than their capabilities permit until they "give up." It hurts the teachers who, unable to bring themselves to make a conscious choice, struggle through the day trying to teach to all levels and doing none well enough.

<u>**And Now the Results Are In**</u>

Inevitably, whenever we proceed incorrectly for long enough, the day of reckoning comes.  That time has arrived, and disaster has befallen our children.

We are the first in the history of our country to be less well educated than the preceding generation. Hundreds of thousands of high-school graduates leave school without being able to read their diplomas.  Also, the Department of Education tells us:

> "Students 20 years behind in learning.  American children are about 20 years behind in their knowledge of math, reading, writing, and science, educators said today in a series of reports that painted a bleak picture of academic achievement nationwide.

> "The Education Department said that, regardless of age, pupils lost ground in achievement levels in math, reading, writing and science between the early 1970s and 1980's.  By 1990, they were back at the same level as in the 1970's, it said.

> "In math, for example, more than 60 percent of children in grades 4, 8 and 12 can perform simple math problems using basic skills.  However, fewer than 20 percent of those in the three grades can tackle solid grade-level work.

> "As for advanced math, the report said 1 percent or less of the fourth-and eighth-graders, and 2.6 percent of high school seniors can work at this level."[1]

In 1983, the National Commission on Excellence in Education issued a report entitled "A Nation at Risk."  It was a warning to the Nation regarding its deteriorating public school system. They found the average achievement of high school students was lower than it was 26 years ago. The report began with the following statement:

"Our Nation is at risk.  Our once unchallenged preeminence in commerce, industry, science, and technological innovation is being overtaken by competitors throughout the world . . .(mostly because) the educational foundations of our society are presently being eroded by a rising tide of mediocrity that threatens our very future as a Nation and a people.

"If an unfriendly foreign power had attempted to impose on America the mediocre educational performance that exists today, we might well have viewed it as an act of war."[2]

This Commission hoped for change and improvement.  There has been change.

In 1983, one indicator of risk stated that in 19 academic tests of international student achievement among industrialized nations, American students never placed first or second.[3]  Now, 14 years later, information from the Third International Mathematics and Science Study (TIMSS), as reported in the National Education Goals Report, 1997, has changed our concern about not placing first or second to a concern that we might not place last.

United States' eighth-graders (those who are on the threshhold of entering high school) rank 25th in math, and 14th in science in the world.[4]  Even with the use of clustering to make us feel better about our scores, we are still pitifully behind.

Another indicator of risk in 1983 stated that 23 million American adults were functionally illiterate.[5]  This statistic, too, has changed. Now, according to a 1993 National Adult Literacy Survey, "About 90 million Americans (55 percent of the adult population) are functionally illiterate."[6]

This is what the system has wrought.  This is what we must change for the sake of our children and grandchildren who will inherit their country in the condition to which we have brought it.

<u>**Goals**</u>

Goals have been written. Goals have been studied. Goals have been revised. Is it not obvious by now to everyone that something further needs to be done? Whereas the goals may be commendable, we need the exact and specific steps that tell us how they are to be accomplished.

For example, in one study, Goal 5 reads as follows, "By the year 2000, United States students will be first in the world in mathematics and science achievement."[7] Great goal. But how exactly do we make it a reality? The truth is, this goal can't be achieved unless we redesign the system. And to do that we must start at the very beginning.

Before I present the specific steps in order to change the system, however, let me share with you the specific steps that brought us to our present condition. There can't be change without full understanding. And there can't be full understanding until we find ourselves in the classroom; until we put ourselves in our children's places.


<u>**The View From the Inside**</u>

I promised to take you inside the elementary classroom so that you might observe firsthand what the system is doing to children. This is not a difficult task except in this respect—trying to describe the faces of the children as they discover and then process the fact that they are failures within the system. It's difficult to describe the look in their eyes as they glance around to see who is watching as they take—what is to them—that long walk to the lowest reading group; as they glance back to see who's watching when they can't answer the questions; or as they look around the room to see who's laughing because they are working in a reader that everyone else in the room finished months ago. Their pain, perplexity and embarrassment are evident. The results of this cruelty—their total loss of dignity—is heartbreaking to watch. And teachers are forced to be perpetrators of this cruelty.

# A Child Created by a Mainstreamed System

Happy and eager to learn, Johnny enters school for the first time.  But almost immediately he realizes that what the teacher is asking of him is much too difficult.  He can't understand any of it.

He cannot hear the sounds and he cannot do the required work in the amount of time allotted.  There must be some explanation.  The teacher is asking too much.  But, thinks Johnny, when she sees that none of the other children can understand it either, she'll slow down.  He looks about for support.  He turns to Billy, who is sitting next to him.  To his surprise, he finds that Billy has not only finished the work but is sitting there head on hand, bored, waiting on him.  And he, Johnny, can't do the work.  He tries to hurry, which somehow seems to delay him further.  Not yet old enough to define failure, he feels it wash over him nevertheless.  And it's not a good feeling.

Johnny wonders how Billy can do the work so quickly when he can't do it at all.  The newborn realization that he is a failure takes root and grows with each addition of new work that he can neither understand nor finish.  The realization becomes a full-blown frustration that grows rapidly, as it is compounded daily.  And now this emotional distress incapacitates him even further.

The teacher is moving about the room, passing out papers.  She lays Billy's paper down and moves on.  Johnny looks over at it.  It's so neat and has two stars on it.  And suddenly he realizes that he doesn't want anyone to see his paper.  He doesn't want to see it himself.  He tries to picture it.  He remembers not knowing how to do some of it.  He remembers having to erase part of it.  Maybe it'll be better than he thinks.

A shadow falls across his desk.  It's her.  He looks at the paper she lays before him.  No, not better than he thought.  It's eraser-smudged and marked with an angry red check minus.  He's not exactly sure what that means, but he can tell it isn't good.  He begins to tremble.  He grabs his paper quickly and tries to cram it into his desk; however it bounces back out and falls to the floor.  He picks it up and tries again but the desk is too full of all the other papers that were supposed to go home and didn't.  He can't let his parents see them, and he can't let the teacher see him throwing them away. He glances up to see if she's watching. She is. His stomach begins to hurt. Will anyone believe him?

But the worst is yet to come. Johnny looks back at Billy, who laughs at him, and the word is passed. Johnny's unaware that there are others just like him in the room because all the important signals come from the Billys and the teacher. So now the whole room knows he's a failure—and soon his whole world.

He can tell the teacher is irritated with him. He can feel it in the reading group also, when he can't hear the sounds so he can say the words. He can see she's struggling to be patient, but he knows that he's disappointing her. Everywhere he goes, he's disappointing someone. And now she's moving more quickly to keep all those who can do the work challenged, to keep her supervisors happy, to keep their quotas met, and to execute the State edicts. More and more unfinished papers lie on his desk. He's forgotten what he's supposed to do on some of them.

When the first report card comes out, Johnny sees that those check minuses have been transposed into F's. He's not too sure what they stand for either, but one thing about them he knows for certain—they enrage parents.

And so he sits six hours a day, five days a week, failing time after time. He begins to dread each day and to hurt in places where he has never hurt before. He decides that trying is too painful. He gives up. And now the only thing he knows for certain is that he hates school. Because now Billy's laughter has segregated him on the playground. He's one of "those."

The years drag on. He is retained once in the primary grades and once during the intermediate grade level. It hurt to fail, but at least Billy has moved on—with honors. No, wait. New Billys have taken his place. But now, they're not only younger than he, they're also smaller. He can't be retained again, he's already two years older than the others. And even though he is now larger, he is no wiser, and sits as ever in the lowest reading group.

Finally, he reaches junior high school, and it gradually dawns on him that he is now old enough to do something about those feelings of frustration and failure that have dogged his every step.

He looks around and finds many choices. For one thing he can feel better about himself through drugs. Man, what a great feeling for the first time in his life! Gone for the moment is that heretofore unshakable feeling of failure and rejection and ridicule. Of course, when the high is over, the low he returns to is even lower than his previous low, but the feeling (while it lasted) was so good that he reaches for it again and again, and then for a way to support the habit.

But drugs are not his only choice. He can erase his feelings of inferiority by becoming a bully. No girl has ever liked him because he was "dumb"; maybe they'll like him if he's brave. Or he can find others like himself and form a gang. His being larger is finally worth something. But alone or united, it's pay-back time, and everyone he hits is a Billy—from the elderly lady he mugs to the parents (among others) he begins to threaten.

Whatever stage in this process these children reach, they all have one thing in common. They believe themselves to be failures and live accordingly. Some try to change it by extreme or violent measures because they've always felt like a nobody wanting desperately to be somebody. Others just settle into that failure mentality, which means their unique talents are lost forever to a country that sorely needs them.

For a better understanding of what a child feels, imagine yourself confined to a chair seven hours a day, five days a week, and never being able to do correctly what is asked of you. Each task is too difficult; yet others all around you are doing them well. In one year's time, what would you believe about yourself? How about in twelve years? Then what have we done to our children?

During my preparation for becoming a teacher, one professor gave us these 26 symbols we had never seen before.

And at the same pace that the system sets for a child who is not ready to learn the letters of the alphabet, the professor then began to put these letters together.  Much too rapidly for us, he began to make words of them that completely confused us.  Also, we were completely unaware that a control group who'd been given the answers was sitting among us.  And then, we became completely embarrassed.  I still remember the frustration we felt.  How could anyone do something so well that seemed so impossible to us.  By the time the professor  gave us a test, we were mentally blocked and wondered if perhaps we were not quite as bright as we'd thought we were.  Even more important, we never wanted to see those silly letters again.

The experience was sobering.  And so it is with your children.  Pushed too early and too fast, they become confused.  Some never come out of it—about 90 million at last count.


## **The Bright Fare No Better**

As Johnny struggles, Billy sits head on hand, watching, waiting, and forming all his future views on learning.  One  mother's complaint is representative of those I heard as a teacher through the years and those I heard in interviews across the country.  She said, "My nine-year-old son will be in the fourth grade this year, but his third grade teacher told me that he will probably not learn very much that he does not already know.  He says school is boring.  Now what do I do?"

When teachers insist on having some "sparkplugs" (brighter students) in their classes, they are not thinking of the children.  This is an example of adult wants taking precedence over children's needs.

> "A study from The National Research Center on the Gifted and Talented at the University of Connecticut showed that a growing number of the nation's most promising students are sitting out their days in boredom.  They are being taught material

they already know.  Bright students tend to achieve less, in relation to their ability, than other youngsters. They learn early on, that if they do well in school, they are simply given extra, dull paperwork.

"Schools actually create, and encourage students to become underachievers who conclude that learning requires no effort or mental rigor and offers no challenge or fascination.  Smart children already know as much as 70 percent of what is being taught in their classrooms."[8]

Mainstreaming teaches children how to "tune out" and let their minds wander when something is being said that they already know. It also teaches them to generalize that all learning is like this.

To address this problem, some schools have "gifted" programs. Whereas these are of some benefit, they do not provide the ideal solution.  One young man explained, "Being bright was a burden in some ways.  For one thing, while I was in the Gifted Program, I missed too much of the basics being taught in my classroom.  We did some neat projects, but that couldn't replace what I was missing."  This presents a problem to classroom teachers.  What do they teach while the remedial readers and gifted students are out of their rooms?

The problem is getting worse.  Wherever textbooks are made easier and more repetitive, the level of teaching in our nation's classrooms will continue to decline.  This has already reached our colleges.

In the 1983 "Nation at Risk Report," the Commission recommended that schools and colleges adopt more rigorous and measurable standards to accompany higher admission requirements and that they have higher expectations for academic performance and student conduct.[9]  This is another expectation that has not only failed to become a reality, but has reversed itself to lower and lower levels.  Some studies show that the mandatory course credits needed to graduate are approximately one-third of what they were in the sixties, and only approximately one-third of the top schools require an English composition course.  Is this not alarming?


## The Middle Child

It is thought that we teach to the middle child, and in many respects, this is true.  Yet mainstreaming does not serve even these children as well as it might.  The middle child's strengths—like those of the brighter children—will go unexplored and unchallenged.  Their weaknesses—like those of the slower children—will go unaddressed.

Author and Parent Consultant Eda LeShan said that educators are like gardeners.  They are respecters of differences, fully aware that they cannot change a rose into a violet.  What concerns them is creating an environment where a rose bush can become its best rose-self, and where a violet can become its best violet-self.[10]  From my experiences and from those of many teachers across the country, we have found that mainstreaming does not create an environment where a child can become his or her best unique self.


## "Our System's Wonderful!"

There are those primary teachers who claim that the system is fine, even wonderful.  I met one such teacher working as a clerk in a store.  She told me she was a primary teacher, working here in the evenings to supplement her income.  I asked her what she thought of the system.  "Wonderful," she said.  Because I was familiar with this particular system and its problems I was taken aback.  Another customer approached the counter, however, so I did not pursue it.

As I browsed the rest of the store, the customer left and the clerk/teacher walked over to me and asked, "Ah, what's the name of your book anyway?"  When I told her she wrinkled her nose and said, "Oh, cute."

I then asked her what she thought of the "whole language" approach to reading that her system was using.

"Not good."

Then I asked if she had any say in changing it for her first graders.

"Well, no."

"How many students per classroom?"

"Thirty."

"What's happening to your bright students?"

"Well, I can't do as much with them as I'd like."

"What about unready children?"

"Not good."

"Self esteem?"

By this time she seemed angry at the system herself, when she said, "It's being absolutely destroyed."  At this she looked down, and although I could not bring myself to say, "So, the system isn't wonderful after all," the words nevertheless seemed to hang almost tangibly in the air between us.

Our system is not wonderful because far too many of today's children are either stressed to the point of damage because they are not ready for the tasks they are asked to perform, or they are bored because they've been ready for some time but must sit and wait for everyone else to become ready.

My classes were always diverse.  For example, one year I had 12 remedial students, 1 genius, 5 advanced students, 1 mentally retarded child, 3 Learning Disabled children, and 8 other students of varying levels of readiness and ability.  Can anyone tell me that each child in this situation (with one teacher) was able to reach their absolute fullest potential in all subjects?


## **Why Continue Mainstreaming?**

> They might not need me — yet they might
> I'll let my heart be just in sight—
> A smile so small as mine might be
> Precisely their necessity—
>
> —Emily Dickinson

We continue to use mainstreaming because the system has forgotten certain things regarding the children. For example, it has forgotten that a child is a complicated, naturally perceptive organism, who absorbs readily, watches with clarity, and processes unerringly. It has forgotten how different the educational, emotional, and physical needs of elementary school children are and how helpless, fragile, and intensely moldable they are at the hands of adults.

Also forgotten is how vital the need is for the promotion and nurture of a healthy self-image in young children, and how necessary this is to the learning process. Forgotten is their radar-like ability to sense rejection, dislike and disapproval. Young children are like soft clay; e.g., everything leaves an imprint—the drawn eyebrows, a frown, harsh words or sarcastic remarks. All are computed by our children. And processed. And stored.

*    *    *

"Nevertheless," say our experts, "we must mainstream. We must put the slower children with brighter students. This is the way they learn."

This is true. They do learn. I watched this learning for seventeen years.

The brighter students learn to be bored and lose interest, and Johnny learns that he cannot begin to do what the other children are doing. He learns that he is inferior in some way—which his grades then affirm. But mostly, mostly he learns that he's a failure and finds that others agree. He is NOT a failure, but you'll never convince him now. Yes, he will learn, but not with pleasure.

Solutions

## l) <u>Search for answers at the PRIMARY elementary level.</u>

Traditionally, we have looked for answers at the intermediate elementary, secondary, and college levels (where the problems are found). We must look for answers where our problems begin, from the first day a child walks into a kindergarten classroom. (Yes, influences on learning begin much earlier in the home, but we have no control over those.)

None of the goals set forth by presidents, governors, national leaders and administrators seem to focus on where we must begin to search for the reasons behind our failures and for the insights to their solutions. The answers begin and lie within the child at the kindergarten level.

## 2) <u>Admit to ourselves that a mainstreaming system does not work.</u>

Based on the statistics cited earlier, it is apparent that our current educational system is not working. When something so critical to a nation's survival is so obvious a failure, it becomes imperative to reevaluate. Have we done that in education? Can we admit now that putting children of all ability levels or those in all different stages of readiness together has helped to bring us to our present condition?

Mainstreaming was brought into being in the hope that children would learn from each other. That has not happened (or has not happened enough) as evidenced by test scores and our standing among other nations. The concept of mainstreaming was supported in some measure so that children who could not do as well as others would be hidden and thus not be embarrassed. That has not happened either. Children are not hidden. And they are embarrassed.

31

That's why, after mainstreaming was instituted, parents began to push teachers to place their child in a higher reading group. This was one of my biggest problems with parents. I explained to them that their child must work from success, not frustration. In most cases, this just didn't matter. "But my child is embarrassed being in the lowest reading group." Of course he's embarrassed. But that's what mainstreaming is. "But my child is not learning anything new; he's bored." Of course he's bored. But that's what mainstreaming produces. "My child is in seventh grade and can't read because somehow he slipped through the cracks in the system." Of course he did. But that's what mainstreaming does.

### 3) **<u>Stop using bright students as "teachers."</u>**

Rather than changing the system that has brought us to this state, many of those in charge have come up with new ideas and philosophies to maintain the status quo. For example, one such philosophy is to leave the system as is and let the bright children teach the slower children. Good teachers know this is a devastating solution.

It is devastating for our bright children, who are losing precious time and motivation. It is devastating for our slower children, who completely lose confidence in themselves. It is devastating for primary educators who know what to change but do not have the power or authority to make these "proper" changes.

Bright students cannot teach slower children for many reasons. Not the least of these is the humiliation the slower children feel having to be taught by someone their own age, from their own class, and (sometimes) by someone physically smaller than they.

During one television program that was promoting this idea, the child being tutored had to sit down by his classmate "teacher." The face of this child gave us the picture as he walked up to his chair and slid into this demoralizing situation.

Another reason this will not work is that a bright child can tell another child what to say or write, but learning to read is a progressive process. You can't pronounce a word if you haven't spent time on each blend, consonant and vowel sound, or the phonetic rules of pronunciation. In a single sitting, no one can bring these children up-to-date on all the sounds that make up a word.

Also, this is a serious infringement on the education of our brighter students. They must be free to work and move at a far different pace, at their own level. They do not have the time to be teachers. They are not qualified to be teachers. It is not their responsibility to be teachers.

Are we now talking only of the public school system? No. Any school system (private, parochial or public) that mainstreams (puts children of all different ability levels and stages of readiness together) is forcing the faster learners to wait on others to grasp what they themselves have known for some time, if not for years.

## 4) **Don't accept mediocrity or failure.  Demand excellence.**

Some parents say, "My children are doing okay in the present system." But that's not enough, is it? Why allow children just to get by when they can be developed to the full extent of their capabilities? If your children are doing "okay" in the present system, they could be doing very well in a redesigned system. On the other hand, children who do very well in today's system may be capable of doing extraordinarily well. Demand nothing less than that.

## 5) **Do not rush or retard the readiness process.**

All of life is process. We cannot force the bud to be a   full-blown flower. We cannot push the caterpillar into being a mature butterfly. We cannot rush the chick from the shell. Rushing the process can destroy the flower, the butterfly and the chick. Do we fear that nothing in all of nature will make it into being unless we intervene?

Seemingly we have learned you cannot rush processes with all else except our children. When I watch parents, teachers, and administrators push children into tasks for which they are not ready, I ask, "What are you afraid of? Do you believe that the children will pass some illusionary point of no return where if they aren't pushed to read before they are capable of reading, they will never read?" This is essentially saying: Unless we begin a task before we are capable of performing it, we shall never be able to perform that task.

For example, if we believe our babies must get an early start on walking or they will never walk, we intervene. Because of this fear, we take our two-month-old babies and begin to work with them. We stand them up, straighten their legs, massage their muscles, and make them practice every day for six hours. And we do this until the child finally learns to walk at about year one, when he or she would have started walking anyway.

They will walk, that is, IF we have not damaged muscle, bone, tendons, cartilage, and psyche. And we have spent nine miserable months, forcing, pushing, pressuring, and manipulating a process that would have occurred naturally and easily when the time was right. In other words, when we intervene and override the readiness process, it is possible to destroy.

Conversely, much will be lost if we try to maintain the status quo within a growth process. For example, we wish to keep the bud a bud and therefore do not place it in the proper setting or give it what it needs to bloom and grow. Thus, we have destroyed all the possibilities and the unique beauty of the flower it could have become, but now never will.

We do this to our bright children when we keep them, for the most part, at the level of every other child in the room. Not that they do not succeed to some measure, but do they succeed to their own level, or merely to a lesser level as what they can do is compromised by what their classmates cannot? How much more could they have grown had they been placed in the right setting and been given what they needed to bloom? How many possibilities and how much unique beauty have been lost. What might they have become, but now never will?

Picture this. Your son, a fourth-grader, learned how to add and subtract in the first and second grades, and how to multiply in the third grade. He's now ready for long division. But half of the students in his class have not yet learned their addition, subtraction, or multiplication facts well enough to proceed. Do you ever wonder what your son is doing while his teacher is teaching addition, subtraction, and multiplication to the other children?

Picture your fifth-grader who learned to read in the first grade. More than half of her classmates are six to seven levels behind her. Do you ever wonder what your daughter is doing while she waits for the others to struggle over each word? Later in this book, children such as she will tell you what they do while they wait.

Here we are retarding the growth process. We are keeping the child at the status quo of 29 other children. Can we even imagine the waste?

It is time to stop retarding the learning process in our children. It is also time to stop rushing it. This brings us to "readiness" and how to provide for it within the classroom.

# Chapter 2

Readiness


The hatred of anything always begins at the point
of frustration.

-A most forgotten, most important
principle of education.


## Readiness

Each year far too many five-year-olds are not ready to begin
kindergarten. What is worse, many school systems begin pre-first-
grade formal instruction in kindergarten rooms where no provision
has been made for the children's different stages of readiness.
Where does this leave the unready?

37

When level of maturity is ignored and chronological age is the sole determining factor, we overlook this inarguable fact—a child cannot do what he or she is not ready to do.  To force these children to perform tasks they are not mature enough to perform will cause problems for them somewhere, sometime in their lives.

In his book, "Stress and Your Child," Dr. Archibald D. Hart cites some chilling statistics.

" -Children as young as five-years-old are developing ulcers.

-Researchers have noted an alarming increase in depression in children all across the nation.

-Increasing numbers of younger adolescents and children are turning to alcohol, drugs, sex, and violence—either as an escape from stress or a way of 'letting off steam.'

-Accidents are the number-one killer of adolescents—stressed adolescents are two-and-a-half times more likely to have an accident.

-The suicide rate for adolescents has tripled since 1958—and younger children are killing themselves."[1]


Stress in school begins when children are expected to do tasks that they are developmentally and physically incapable of doing.  I have watched this process.  When passing kindergarten rooms, I saw teachers sitting out in the hall with one child at a time, holding flashcards of math facts, letters, and words.  Many children struggled tearfully because they could not name the figures or words on the cards but they knew that some of their classmates could.  They returned to their room in disgrace and they didn't know why.  How could these five-year-olds understand the concept of readiness when many adults evidently don't.  This approach forces teachers to be the perpetrators of a crime against children, and they are given nine months to bring each class of the unready to grade level.


### That's Not the Way I Heard It.

My primary Elementary Education Professor "enthusiastically" loved children.   Her deep and full understanding of how young children develop, grow, and learn  touched her students.  However, most of the teaching strategies designed for young children that I learned in her classes proved impossible to implement in today's system. This, of course, evokes the dichotomous force (what the young child needs versus wrong procedures) that has, among other things, caused almost half of our adult population to be functionally illiterate.


## What Was I Taught?

It's supposed to be a happy time. To a five-year-old, each day is one of wonder and discovery, filled with new things to see, new words to use, new ideas to try. No day is long enough to see and do it all, and tomorrow seems so far away. Children of this age are physically active and their large muscles cry out for activity. They are emotional and demand affection and attention. They need outlets for self-expression, opportunities to please, and moments when they can gain status.

Once this was a happy time, when children could enjoy their age of wonder and discovery. Today, however, it is not an age of wonder and discovery, but one of confusing signs and strange figures to recognize on paper—not new ideas to try, there's no time.

The powerful desire of young learners to please is frustrated whenever what they are able to do falls light years short of what the teacher is ordered to expect of them. They will be frustrated whenever, instead of being active, they are required to sit and do fine detailed work with small finger muscles that are not fully developed. They gain status, but in the wrong direction. Instead of affection, they receive disapproval. The pressure turns little stomachs to rebellion. This was supposed to have been a happy time, but it isn't.

> "The Play Schools Association published a booklet in 1963 which read in part: 'Being a child isn't what it used to be. Huck Finn is a delinquent, Tom Sawyer isn't working up to capacity, and Heidi is in foster care. Jim Hawkins is too young to be a

cabin boy, and whoever would let Alice just sit there,
doing nothing at all but dream through a summer
afternoon? . . . .

"Today's child often walks a tightrope between
neglect and pressure.  He gets too much stimulation
or none at all.  He may have forgotten how to play
. . . parents worry whether children will excel before
they have left kindergarten.'"[2]

Yes, pressure, tightropes, and stress for our five-year-olds are the
order of the day.  If this was a concern for our children in 1963,
what would the writers of this article think now that this problem
has been magnified many times over?

One school district purchased a reading program for
kindergarten that consisted of stories using small words such as
hit, bit, sit, and fit, and every child in the room was forced to try to
read from this series.  Nothing could have been more difficult for
many of these children.  Their teachers reported a record number
of stomachaches that year.  Showing me the books, the teachers
asked in dismay, "What in the world are we doing to our children?"

We knew that whoever within this particular system had chosen
this series, approved it, and forced teachers to use it for all children
at the same pace, knew very little of what was correct and proper
training for the safe growth and development of the five-year-old.
But that's another chapter.


## "What in the World Are We Doing to Children?"  The Doctors Tell Us

In his book, "Why Johnny Can't Read," Rudolf Flesch spoke
of readiness as the "holy of holies," and the "inner sanctum" of the
science of reading.  He said one expert, who wrote an entire book
on the subject of reading readiness, never once defined it.  "So,"
said Mr. Flesch, "I'll offer my own definition.  Reading readiness
means the readiness of the teacher to let the children start reading."[3]

While I'm certain that Mr. Flesch's definition of readiness was tongue-in-cheek, he does present us with a prevalent point of confusion that prevails today.

During some of my early interviews and conversations, I sensed a slight reluctance to discuss "readiness," which I found puzzling because it is such a vital concept in the education of young children. Finally, one woman made the connection. She explained, "When you said 'readiness,' I thought you were referring to some more expensive government programs to prepare children to begin school." When I understood what the problem was, I could explain that I was not discussing programs.

Too often we ascribe to readiness a meaning that includes only something another person can do for the child—for example, a good breakfast, the proper rest, responsible parenting, or yet another government program. Whereas these may be commendable aids to the preparedness of a child to learn, the readiness I speak to is that physiological development within the actual physical bodies of children—that which no one else can do for them.

I was luckier in my research for a definition of readiness than was Mr. Flesch. Dr. Robert Gregory, pediatrician, explained, "Normally the nervous system of a five-year-old is not fully developed. The neuronal pathways from the eyes and ears to the brain may not be set, not fixed. Also, the eye muscles that track during reading and the part of the brain that helps us focus on a sound and then translates that sound into a word may not be fixed in many children. The area of the brain that converts auditory stimuli into verbal results may as yet be immature.

"The part of the brain that screens out excess sounds may also be immature. Therefore, not only are many of our children struggling to concentrate on advanced work for which they are not ready, but they can't screen out background noises. This makes it even more difficult for the child to assimilate the incoming information. It is possible that these neuronal pathways are not set in the five-year-old."[4]

If the pathways are not mature, children should not be pushed into reading. We must not push auditory discrimination, rush visual recognition or force little eyes to track small letters before the physiological capability exists.

Because vision is not normally yet mature, the child should be protected from activities that call for frequent refocusing of the eyes. It is better to provide rest periods and quiet times alternated with periods of activity.

My internist agreed with Dr. Gregory and added, "And don't forget the immune system. It's not mature either. Stress raises the white blood count. Distressed children who work under pressure will have more colds, infections, and illnesses." The physicians I interviewed agreed that this process of pushing children toward tasks for which they are not ready damages them, and the "tummyaches" have increased in direct proportion to the pushing.

Readiness then, occurs when the child's system is physiologically capable of embracing the skills for learning to read without being frustrated and inevitably, without being made to feel like a failure. So, as we proceed with the proper care and education of the five-year-old, armed now with a definitive understanding of readiness, let us take great care to ascertain the readiness status of five-year-old children before we seat them in a classroom and begin formal  reading, math and writing instruction. When we ignore this most crucial concept we enable our children to dread the coming school years rather than to look forward to them.


## "I Hate School!"

When kindergarten becomes an unhappy, stressful place, hatred of school and learning begins. We have forgotten that the hatred of anything always begins at the point of frustration. With each passing year, I found more and more children entering my first- or second-grade rooms disliking school.

As children progress through the first and second grades the standards they set for themselves often exceed their abilities. We begin to see many holes erased in their papers and much paper crumpling. Some have called this the "eraser age." This behavior is another indication that the child is now aware of criticism from peers or adults. They begin to see that the world is no longer made just for them alone but for their clasmates as well. What others think of them begins to influence their feelings, beliefs, and actions.

Far too often schools become places where little egos are first crushed, where eagerness dies, where poor self images are born, where children learn to be failures, and where they develop dysfunctional coping behaviors that follow them into the rest of their lives. I believe that a love of learning is crucial to the learning process. However, both the love of learning and learning itself are lost under pressure and stress. Pushing harder and harder unready children who are sitting among ready children will only compound the problem tenfold. In this case, the old saying is true—"The hurrier I go, the behinder I get."

Someone once came up with a beautiful picture of what teaching kindergarten should be: "It's like trying to keep 30 corks under water all at the same time." It is understood that one would neither be able nor want to do this. Unfortunately for our young children, the system has found a way to do it.


## Is This What the Founder of Kindergarten Had in Mind?  Not Even Close.

Friedrich Froebel, a German educator, introduced the idea of a school for early childhood education—the kindergarten, or child's garden. It emphasized games, play, songs, and crafts.

Froebel's kindergarten curriculum had as its objective the cultivation of the child's self-development, self-activity, and socialization. Like Johann Heinrich Pestalozzi, with whom he studied, Froebel protested vigorously against teaching children ideas that they did not understand. He also accepted the Pestalozzian concept which stressed the importance of emotional security for the child.

## The Promotion of Readiness

Kindergarten was designed to be a place for the promotion of readiness. The criteria are security, happiness, activity, balance, imaginative expression, sociability, and FUN. Ideally, kindergarten should be a place for running, playing, pretending, being expressive, being creative, and playacting, while little muscles and neuronal pathways are maturing.

"But my child is ready," you say. Perhaps. Perhaps not. Remember, readiness is not something you do. It's not something you can rush. It's not something you can fix or alter. It's not something you can program, and it's not something you can see. There is no way to know exactly what is going on in a small child's emotional makeup until symptoms appear.

Remember from Chapter 1 how much a child can feel and perceive? They can sense their parent's anxiety that they read as soon as possible, and little children strive to please these adults who want to move them along quickly to the next stage. This is another adult want that affects what a child needs. Sometimes the parents' anxiety stems from not wanting their children to be behind those of a neighbor, a relative, or a friend. More often, however, parents are caught between what their child can do and what the system demands. Whatever the case, the damage is the same.

Such damage is rarely seen until it is too late. Even if children develop a visible nervous tic, have stomachaches or headaches, become a discipline problem, have trouble sleeping, or suddenly experience a personality change, this is seldom attributed to the fact that they are not ready for the tasks they are being pushed to perform. All the children who are rushed into tasks inappropriate for their individual stage of readiness are the children who may suffer burn-out later on, may develop emotional problems that will be apparent when they're older, or may join millions of children who have diagnosable psychological problems that need treatment by a mental health professional.

## When Then?

There are two main schools of thought on when a child is ready to receive formal reading and math instruction.  One group says that girls are not normally ready to hear and discern phonetically until they are six or six and a half, and boys are not always ready until they are six and a half or seven.  They maintain that the preschooler who is pushed ahead does not always stay ahead.  This group says those studies designed to prove that pre-first-grade formal instruction is effective are inconclusive because this research does not tell the whole story concerning the emotional effects of early reading instruction.  They cite the studies that checked the progress of early readers in upper grades and found that even though these children did maintain their lead in primary grades, that lead disappeared or decreased in the intermediate grades.

The supporters of the other school of thought maintain that as far as formal instruction goes—the earlier the better.  If children are not ready, they won't learn until they are.


## So!  How Do We Reconcile the Two?

In a mainstreamed system where children of all abilities sit together, we don't.  The problem lies with the system of placing the unready child who needs to begin in a readiness book or a pre-primer in the same room as the child capable of reading at a second grade level.  The first school of thought—which stressed that children who are pushed to read before they can hear the sounds may actually lose ground because of emotional damage—is absolutely true.  I am a witness to the truth of this damage.  The second school of thought—that children who are physically ready can begin formal instruction—may also be true.  The problem is— you can't address both schools of thoughts simultaneously in the same classroom.

Unready children cannot sit in the same classroom with ready children.  It's like mixing oil and water—the water loses its ability to support life, and the oil loses its ability to protect.  When ready children and unready children are mixed, each will cause the other to lose their ability to learn well, if at all.


## <u>The Defenders of Mainstreaming Versus Readiness</u>

The parents who opt for mainstreaming are dealing with a society that (for some inexplicable reason) must attach labels and nicknames, a society that believes ability limitations are synonymous with failure. Is it any wonder then, that parents want their child hidden among a nonhomogeneous group of children? They have been sold on the idea that, if allowed to sit with brighter students, their child will absorb, through some mysterious process similar to osmosis, the same knowledge as the bright. Are our failure rates great enough by now to show us that this is either not happening at all, or not frequently enough?

Children may look at or even copy another child's paper, but this is not learning. Since they are not ready for the task they are copying, they will not always be able to assimilate the information, much less be able to reproduce it later on their own. Mostly what they absorb in this setting is how others see them. They also learn how to copy.

The teachers who lose sight of why they decided to become a teacher in the first place do not want to teach a class of slower children. I hope this reluctance is the result of traditionally being given 30 of these children at a time, along with the same curriculum, expectations, and time schedule as the other teachers.

I also hope that, with a system change and no interference, a teacher would look upon it as a high calling to teach a group of 15-20 such children who are all at the same stage of readiness, have similar abilities and can move at the same pace. Such a situation would allow the teacher to concentrate and apply all of his or her energies and creativity toward moving the children along as quickly as their readiness level permits and then to watch them revel in the success of learning each new thing. Out of view of the watching brighter students and away from the pressure and stress of having to perform at impossible levels, children could relax.  Here they could be successful.  This is when learning becomes a pleasure.

The good teacher can foster a spirit of "this is our team" and take each success and build on it.  For example, when you are happy because you have just succeeded at something important to you, isn't that a time when you believe you can conquer the whole world?  A good teacher knows that the absolutely best time to introduce the next new concept is when a child has that wonderful feeling of success.

It is imperative that our children become happy, productive members of society.  Of lesser importance is which classroom children sit in or what they are called.  Yes, I know about labels.  In any case, it is far less damaging to be called something occasionally from outside a classroom of close-knit peers where one is constantly succeeding than to be laughed at constantly within a mainstreamed classroom where one is constantly failing.

The two prerequisites for a new system are (1) children must work from the seductive pull and thrill of success rather than failure, and (2) adults will understand that all children cannot work at the same pace and thus will not require the exact same course of study.

It is time to look at mainstreaming and its success rate.  This brings us to the next defenders of the current system.

Many administrators, educators, State officials, and politicians who are in charge say it would be far too difficult to change the system, the cost would be prohibitive, and the only way to group children is to rely on inaccurate, culturally biased tests.  Actually, just the opposite is true.  It will not be difficult to change the system; the redesigned system will cost less than the present system; and testing is unnecessary in grouping children, as you will see in the solutions that follow.


## **<u>Will This Redesigned System Work?  Absolutely!</u>**

It worked before.  I interviewed many teachers who grouped children by ability and readiness in the past, as had I.  They all agreed that their success rates far exceeded those in their mainstreamed classrooms, even though they still had too many students at a time.  Imagine how successful they could be with smaller classes.

I asked one group of first-grade teachers what they believed to be the main reason for their success.  "The children were quite ready for each task they were given.  And in their classroom there was no one looking and laughing at them.  We made it possible for them to bloom and grow, and they did."  Asked if they thought it would work again today they responded, "Absolutely!  Our children have not changed physically as far as needing to be ready.  They still mature or don't mature in their own time.  They still learn in the same way.  Their natures and growth patterns have not changed.  The only thing that has changed is the educational system which the adults have changed for reasons we simply cannot imagine."

It also works today.  I have visited schools where grouping is practiced, discipline is enforced, and phonics are taught.  In these schools, children read.

In mainstreamed classes we are doing and will continue to do irreparable damage to many of our children.  When children enter school for the first time it is true that, in large measure, their self-esteem has already been formed by their experiences to-date and by their family—in many cases negatively.  For this reason, it is even more imperative, that the school experience be designed to enhance their self-esteem rather than to lower it.  From this point on, self-esteem will be affected positively by what the children can achieve in their classrooms or destroyed by what they cannot.

*    *    *

Recently, I tutored a five-year-old while his parents looked for a new home in the city to which they were being transferred.  Wondering what "work" a kindergartner could have, I was horrified to discover that it consisted of phonics sheets I had used in second grade.  One blend he was expected to hear involved a third-grade, age-eight skill.  This five-year-old simply could not hear these sounds yet.

When he arrived in his new school district, his teacher was also horrified.  "He can't read!  He can't do subtraction!  Whatever has he been doing?" she asked.  She insisted that the boy be tested so she could address this unbelievable situation, a five-year-old who could not read or do mathematics.  And so, to please this new "excellent" system, this bright, eager, happy, confident five-year-old will have to work all summer trying to adapt to the system.  But the question is:  Come next spring, will he be a bright, eager, happy, confident six-year-old?

## 1)  <u>Accept children exactly where they are in their individual, NATURAL, stage of development.</u>

We must accept children's abilities and limitations whatever that might mean to us personally as parent, teacher, or administrator. This solution is the foundation for all others.  It is also the most difficult, because our tendency is to glance over this statement and then look for something far more substantial.  This is too elemental. We've heard it before.  Besides, doesn't everyone already automatically accept their children?  I'm afraid not.

Our acceptance levels often tend to be in direct proportion to our children's ability and performance levels.  On the surface we may appear to accept children with limitations, but we have not made the proper provisions for them, perhaps because we find it painful to look at them realistically.  Nevertheless, for whatever reason, from all quarters, we hide them in large classrooms and believe we are hiding their limitations as well.  If we sincerely want to help the children and allow ourselves to be entirely honest, we shall admit that this has been more for our sake than for theirs.

Unless we study this solution carefully and apply it to our situations honestly, despite whatever pride we may have to swallow, there will be no changes for the children.  The rule is this:  We take all children individually, at exactly their unique stages as far as we can academically, physically, socially, emotionally and mentally— HAPPILY!

We cannot do this, however, until we change the system.


## 2) <u>Redesign the present educational system to meet the needs of children.</u>

We are forcing children to adapt to a system rather than designing a system to adapt to children.  As it now stands, the system is designed for everyone but the children. (You will see this more fully in future chapters.) The designers of our current system place children of all abilities together in large classes and contend that they will learn to the limit of their capabilities. It just won't happen.

Picture this. A child in a readiness book or first pre-primer sits next to a child ready for a third-grade reader. (Yes, the disparities can be this great or greater.) Picture yourself as the teacher in this classroom, trying to teach both of these children the same math, language, spelling, science, social studies, and health lessons.

The first step in redesigning the system is to group together those children who are in like stages of readiness. The key (forgotten) element here is that children must always work in a group where they can succeed. We must never allow a child to work at the point of frustration. If the work is too difficult and the child is upset, it's the wrong group. If the child is bored, it's the wrong group.

"Yes, but we've tried grouping before and it didn't work!" Then at that time the teachers had no support and no help, or they didn't like grouping and therefore didn't try to make it work. Perhaps they didn't teach phonics, or they were poor teachers. Maybe those doing the research testing didn't like grouping. Mostly what happens, however, is that teachers are given 30 to 40 children at a time, or they are expected to bring their class (regardless of readiness levels) to the same level as the other classes, or the same teachers are assigned the slower class with too many children year after year. We must return to the successful system of grouping and, with the help of good teachers and administrators with vision, teach phonics in smaller classes.


3) **<u>Lower class size.</u>**

In the redesigned system, class size will be reduced to 16 to 20 students. The rule is: The greater the need, the smaller the class. (Yes, we will have the money. In Chapter 6 you will see how to cut back the system by using a very new and novel idea—most of the money will be spent on the children.)

In large classes, the system operates with an assembly-line mentality in which we force-feed facts and then test to see how many facts children can reproduce on tests. That's all teachers have time for. In assembly-line learning, teachers do not have time to teach 30 to 40 children of such diverse abilities to THINK. In a redesigned system with smaller classes, teachers will no longer have five or six reading groups. Therefore, they can give considerable additional time to finding creative ways to teach children not just to regurgitate facts, but to think, to problem-solve, and to reason.

One parent told me he sold his home and moved to another school district because his son, who was making D's and F's, was in such large classes. After the move, this boy (now in smaller classes) began to make A's and B's. Think what he could have done had he been grouped properly as well.

Also, smaller classes will allow the teacher to consider learning styles. This is, of course, an impossibility in a mainstreamed classroom where there is not time to develop  children to be all they can be, much less teach to the way each child learns best—be it auditory (hearing), visual (seeing), tactile (touching), kinesthetic (body movement), or various combinations of the preceding.

In one district, primary teachers were given tests to determine their learning styles. I was definitely not an auditory learner. (Well see, I knew something was wrong.) I was surprised, however, to see just how difficult it was for me to learn the new information being presented solely auditorily. Just imagine, then, how difficult and crippling this is for young children. Learning styles can be addressed in smaller classrooms.


## 4) <u>__Allow Primary teachers to group children.__</u>

Grouping our children correctly does not require the use of expensive, culturally biased, inaccurate tests. Such requirements preclude the use of our very best grouping resource, the primary teacher.

While I was teaching, it became quite clear to me in the first week of school what reading level each child was going to need. Teachers have been reluctant to say this because they feared being criticized. Somehow, society has come to believe that primary elementary teachers don't know as much as teachers in upper grades because it doesn't take a whole heck of a lot to teach kindergarteners or first graders. This is another major fallacy.

One superintendent said to me, "Since you're a new teacher, we'll put you in the first grade, you know, start you off nice and easy." This is the fallacy that has brought us to the point where primary teachers are afraid to speak up and say, "Placing children is no problem. I'll know almost  immediately where they will work to their capacity easily and happily—and successfully." And they will.

"But can't teachers be wrong in their decisions on grouping?" This would have to be a pretty poor teacher. Actually, even without teacher training, couldn't almost anyone working with a small group of children in a reading circle be able to tell when a child is struggling and unable to keep up with the other children?

In the present system, should a teacher be wrong in deciding where to place a child, that decision stands for a whole year. I once took over a class at midyear, and on the first day I realized that two children reading in a middle group were misplaced. After waiting long enough to make certain, I moved them to the top reading group, and even there they quickly surpassed all the other students. In a redesigned system, these two children would have been out of my class at that point and put into the next level group which moved much more quickly. This type of mistake is rare, but I had replaced a new teacher. The point is, however, that the mistake was caught only because of a midyear teacher change, which is also rare.

A redesigned system will include constant checks and balances. For one thing, groupings will not be set in concrete as they are now. If the teacher responsible for the original grouping miscues, or if a child matures greatly over the summer, the next teacher will know early on that this child should be in a different group. Or if everything suddenly begins to fall into place for a child, he or she can be moved into a room nearer his or her new ability level. This new system is fluid.

This redesigned system also prevents the practice of stacking classes—an age-old problem for excellent teachers. Stacking happens when principals put problem children, children of friends and Board members, children with difficult parents, a large number of remedial readers and L.D. (Learning Disabled) children, and children with severe discipline problems all together in one teacher's room because she's the best teacher in the grade level. Yes, the principal has the best interests of the children at heart, but this can happen to good teachers year after year until they are too weary to continue.

## 5) <u>Preserve, protect, and defend a child's state of simplicity.</u>

In many ways today's educational system ravages the two most imperative requirements for happiness. The system undermines the children's confidence, and destroys their state of simplicity— that simplicity which keeps them free to be happy long enough to build a strong base for withstanding the stresses of adulthood.

There are many phases of childhood. Children must be allowed their full time in each one of them. Instead, they are shoved into stresses before they are allowed just to be children.

> "It always grieves me to contemplate the initiation of children into the ways of life when they are scarcely more than infants. It checks their confidence and simplicity, two of the best qualities that heaven gives them, and demands that they share our sorrows before they are capable of entering into our enjoyments."
>
> — Charles Dickens

## 6) <u>Kindergarten and pre-first-grade formal instruction.</u>

Frobel's kindergarten was a place to stimulate the young child's imagination, to provide social contact, and to develop physical and motor skills, coordination and physical dexterity. Kindergarten was designed to be a place to promote readiness while fiercely protecting and providing for the emotional security of the child. Frobel's kindergarten was to be "a child's garden" not an adult proving ground.

Now, after having said that, when children are believed to be ready to move ahead and pre-first-grade instruction is begun, then let everyone proceed with extreme caution. Let everyone keep uppermost in their minds the possible negative effects such "rushing" may have on children, effects that may not show up until much later in a child's life. Let everyone keep uppermost in their minds the various needs and the delicate, fragile, tender age of the five-year-old.


## 7) <u>**Stop the labeling.**</u>

We are a society that lives under the compulsion to label and to attach nicknames to almost everyone. In so doing, we are also teaching our children to label and attach nicknames. We like those television programs in which the main character uses outrageous labels; we claim this helps us to see labeling in its true light, and will help us not to label. Do our children understand this?

We believe our children to be sieves, and that everything we say and do—even though our children are watching—will pass right through them and not be retained. Actually, children more closely resemble sponges. This is what we have missed as a society, and we are paying the price.

As we change the system to educate to differences rather than sameness, we must introduce our children to the Snowflake Theory. We admire the fact that each snowflake is different, but we have not only failed to determine this about our children, we have failed to teach them the concept. Actually, some classtime should be devoted to these differences. Children should be taught that we do not mature at the same rate, and that being different is good, not "bad" or "stupid." How sorely our country needs this philosophy taught—from the cradle to graduation.

Children learn exactly what adults teach and live before them. If the children can learn these labels and exactly where to apply them, they can also learn about late-bloomers and pace. For children to stop labeling, however, adults must stop labeling. Barring that, let us do the next best thing.

Labeling is the excuse most often used for not grouping children where they can succeed. "Other children will laugh at them. They will be labeled." I ask these people, "Where do you think these children are sitting now? Do you believe they are hidden or disguised in those mainstreamed classrooms? Do you believe they sit in isolation booths? If we group by ability, do you believe that children will be able to pinpoint which rooms are which more readily than they can decipher this information right before their very eyes in their mainstreamed classrooms as they watch the slower children struggle through reading books that they themselves zipped through months ago?"

What it comes down to is determining how long the children must endure the labeling and where they will best develop the ego strength base to withstand it. In a redesigned system that places them in a small class of like peers, no laughing or ridicule will occur during all their class time because they are unable to answer a question. Nor will they be labeled as the one who never gets his or her work done. And they will not be reading in the group that 29 other children know is the lowest.

Some teachers, against all good advice, give their reading groups animal names such as Bears, Birds, Butterflies, and Bunnies. While on playground duty, one little girl said that in her class she was in the dumb Bunnies' Group. The tragedy here is that she believed this label that came from her mainstreamed classroom—that same classroom where everyone believes she is safely tucked away, hidden among the other students, learning, and therefore developing a healthy self-image.

In our present system, many children sit in failure and ridicule seven hours a day. In a redesigned classroom of peers, where they are working from success, children are building ego strengths seven hours a day, which will provide them with a firm base for anything they must face outside the classroom.

While in a room where one is constantly succeeding, a child can handle a label when it occurs now and then. The key is that children work from success. If they are succeeding, they can live with an occasional insult because they won't believe it. If they are failing, such insults are the final blow because they do believe them. With regard to failure, the redesigned system totally eliminates the need for retention, which is the most labeling and devastating failure of all to a child, one that everyone not only believes, but remembers.

Does this system do away with grade levels? Not at all. There will still be six grade levels in elementary school. But each grade will include different levels. At the end of sixth grade, all sixth-graders will not be reading at the same level, but they will be reading or will have progressed as far as possible within their learning capabilities.


## Some Last Thoughts

It is time to stop looking for that one, great, deeply philosophical, NEW idea that will whisk away (as if by magic) all our educational woes and provide a solution that in a week's time, will miraculously (and with minimum effort) make our educational system perfect. Yes, we know this one new answer will be costly, but we'll just bite the bullet, raise taxes one more time, and then be finished with our educational problems.

Several school systems thought they had found this "new and right" idea. They spent millions of dollars for computers and all types of the latest technological equipment. They were appalled when test scores continued to fall. The scores did not improve because, whereas technological equipment can be of some limited help, this was the only change made in these systems. No one, great, new idea exists and being new doesn't always mean it's right or even good. The throwing together of all children, regardless of readiness, was once a new idea.

The reasons for our educational predicament are numerous, as are the solutions. In some instances we must return to the old ideas that worked, eliminate new ideas that haven't, understand that right changes are not all that difficult or costly to implement, and begin to look beyond this moment in time. We must stop being so overly concerned now about appearances if we group our children so they can learn, and be far more concerned about later when these children could reach the seventh grade and not be able to read.

Of major importance, we must stop putting people in charge who do not fully understand the needs of primary children and will not listen to the teachers who do. This brings us to administrators.

# Chapter 3

Administrators:  "How Did Our System Get This Bad?"


> "The trouble with tyranny is that the ship of state exists for the sake of the officers; the trouble with democracy is that while the ship is supposed to exist for the sake of the passengers, it really operates best for the benefit of the crew.  And the trouble with the present-day educational system is that it exists for the edification and benefit of the administrators."[1]
>
> — Sydney J. Harris


The question of the decade seems to be, "How did our educational system ever get this bad?"  A good question.  Much of its answer must be laid at administrative doors, for Federal, State, and local administrators, leaders, and "experts" can be the teachers' greatest source of stress and one of the reasons they cannot teach effectively.


## Who Knows?  Evidently Only the Shadow.

Whereas many school officials may be caught within a system that requires them either to "go along" or leave, others are both the designers and the champions of the system.  Neither group seems able to answer the question, "How did the educational system get this bad?"

Members of the bureaucracy from state legislative levels to local school districts, can neither explain it nor offer any clue as to how to fix it, partially perhaps, because to do so would directly affect their own rank and file.  Administrators would have little incentive to look for a solution that could seriously lower the number of administrative personnel they supervise or possibly even to be forced to admit that their own positions are unnecessary.

Whenever teachers have tried to find answers to their question— "Who came up with this idea that prevents us from teaching as children need to be taught, so we can appeal it?"—they have encountered blank stares, finger-pointing and shrugs. After running around in a circle of futility, they have found that administrators at all levels considered themselves innocent. All is left to supposition then, that the requirements, restrictions, and new "bad" ideas that so hamper the teacher must have come into being somewhat along the lines of the "big bang" theory.


## What Those Outside the Classroom Say

When state legislators saw the results of the ninth-grade proficiency tests in one state, some of them decided they needed professional people to explain what was happening.  Some officials of the State Education Department, the very ones who laid down time restrictions, curriculum demands, and the mountains of paperwork that paralyze the teacher, were equally perplexed. Some of them, along with legislators, wondered aloud in interviews how education had gotten in its present condition.

In the individual districts, local administrators either had no answers or would not give the teachers any that went against their own best interests. Disgruntled Board members, however, were not so reticent. Some of them saw what teachers have seen for years—a duplication of function at astronomical prices.

Overall, however, each group seems to be blaming someone else for the problem. Board members blamed the state for too much interference. Superintendents blamed the state for too much paperwork and too many restrictions. The state laid the blame at local administrative doors.

One State official told me that the State board sends  out questionnaires to local school districts asking what their problems are and why education is in such a mess. "We are told," he said, "that the problems are due to local administrators."

Often times State officials will speak in Parent/Teacher Forums. In one such meeting, a teacher asked about the rules, regulations, and restrictions set by the State. An official answered that they came from those teachers whom the State Board interviews. Then they are rubber-stamped within the State Board's parameters. When asked if all grade levels were represented, he answered, "Yes."

I could not believe that kindergarten and first- and second-grade teachers would set such unproductive standards, time limits, and restrictions for themselves and their children. Would a primary teacher suggest or offer any plan that let other subjects take so much time from reading instruction in the early grades? After the meeting I questioned him further but he reiterated, "All grades participate and the teacher's ideas are considered if they are within the Board's parameters." I understood this dilemma.

Local school districts also have parameters. In one district I was asked to help choose new textbooks. I worked all the hours necessary to study the different textbooks from various publishers. I made my decision and went to the supervisor's meeting only to find that the supervisor also had choices. The teachers were quite free to choose—but within the parameters of the supervisor's choices.

This reminded me of the story of the puppies who were let out of a small enclosure as they matured, only to find themselves in a fenced-in yard. Although they were freer than before, they were still enclosed.

This is the round-robin rhetoric, however, that discloses that no one is willing to take any responsibility. Unfortunately, it also shows us that those making the rules are not always working together.

As far as I can determine there are no cohesive or collaborative forces at work. Rather, everyone seems to be working at cross purposes. If the State is making rules and the local administrators are making rules, and if they are not coordinating those rules, you can see how confusing and detrimental a process this is for teachers and for children. Meanwhile, most of those involved in a school district, especially the teachers, agree that they are chafing under burdens of responsibility that get heavier each year, burdens that come from—wherever.

Regardless of who blames whom, none of them can deny certain things. In some systems, the state mandates the amount of time teachers in the first and second grades are required to spend on, for example, science, social studies, and health. In some states, far too much valuable time was given to these subjects at the expense of reading instruction. First- and second-grade teachers asked that reading be made a first priority in these first two all-important grades, they asked for freedom to "work in" these other subjects as time allowed. This request was repeatedly denied or ignored.

In most districts where I've worked, teachers must fill out schedule cards at the beginning of each school year. On these cards they list all the subjects and the exact number of minutes given to each subject according to the State's allotted time requirements for reading, language arts, math, social studies, health, science, art, music, and physical education. Schedules for these subjects must then be worked around special services' classes, lunch, two recesses, miscellaneous duties (lunch money collection, etc.), and special programs.  If a teacher believes in two reading groups a day for primary children (morning groups to provide technical instruction from the adopted reading series; afternoon groups to provide extra reading practice), this valuable time cannot be found.

Here is the dilemma.  The teachers who meet with each reading group twice a day produce the best readers.  In the primary grades, however, in a mainstreamed system, teachers may have up to five or six different reading groups (they may need more).  This means that it's possible to have two reading times for each group only by fudging on State time requirements.  Should a supervisor walk in at the time the schedule listed science but some interruption in the day's schedule had occurred, or there had been a great creative moment in a reading group and the teacher had prolonged it, that teacher was written up on an evaluation form as not having followed the schedule.  I was told by supervisors, "State officials can walk in at any time.  You'd better be working on the subject scheduled at that time and be giving it its full time allotment."

This, of course, plays into one of the many vicious circles found in education today.  Children cannot read well enough to study, for example, their science books, so they fail their exams on this subject.  Desperate officials then require that science be pushed down into even earlier grades and given additional time, which takes more time from reading instruction.  The result—children are unable to read their science books.

A teacher in one state told me she wrote a protest letter to her State Department of Education. The letter closed by saying, "We realize it is your right to have some input as to our curriculum, but please give teachers the freedom in early grades to teach reading first and foremost."  The State Department closed their letter with an answer that was brief, succinct and cut right to the heart of it: "Yes, it is our right."

## Show Us How to be Called On, Arnold Horshak

In an attempt to find answers for educational dilemmas, another vicious circle begins when these same administrators and "experts" are asked for answers. Many times their answers consist of hiring yet another expert to find out what's wrong. In many districts already overburdened and top-heavy with administrators, this has been the solution.

Think of it as a surrealist classroom filled with teachers and administrators mainstreamed together. The question is asked, "What is wrong with education?" Like Arnold on "Welcome Back, Kotter," teachers who know the answer raise their hands, very eager to respond, but the system calls only on the administrators.

The following are some of the strange beliefs advanced by the system:

1.  The more administrators cost, the better they are.

2.  The more administrators you have, the better the system.

3.  The more complex the title, the greater the wisdom of the title-holder.

4.  The longer the term of contract, the better theadministrator.

None of these is necessarily so.


## Chain of Command

When you think of some form of chain of command, you usually think of someone reporting to a supervisor who reports to a manager, and so on up the line to a chief executive. In many school systems, however, a teacher may have as many as three, or four immediate supervisors. Depending on the particular system, teachers may report to a principal, an assistant principal, one or several assistant superintendents, and an immediate supervisor. In some cases, there is a supervisor of supervisors through whom teachers have to go to get children placed correctly. In some districts, personnel directors oversee the teachers and often have say over the placement of the children.

Not even big business could stand up under the burden of such expense. Instead, some businesses are eliminating layers of personnel, and reducing management to cut costs, increase profits, and provide large bonuses for those in charge. But a school district has no profits and no bonuses.

Superintendents gain much of their status and prestige (and sometimes a larger salary) by the number of administrators they manage. This explains two things: 1) why some superintendents keep on hiring administrators even in the face of school-district bankruptcy, and 2) where much of the money goes. Some districts may have only the administrators they need. Some districts, however, have so many administrators that the teachers and children are crushed into immobility by the very weight of them.


## That's Not All

Some state laws bar school districts from reassigning any administrator to a job with lesser pay or responsibility. One Board member admitted to me that it's quite a problem for his district because they've been sued for this several times. So in these cases, instead of being dismissed, incompetent administrators either get promoted or are given lateral moves. Teachers know this is true. Such people become their superiors!

For example, one district found it necessary to remove two principals from their positions. Since they could not be "demoted" to the classroom, jobs were invented for them. They were given lateral moves with the title "assistant superintendent," and two new principals were hired. This district that had run beautifully for years with one superintendent, now had a superintendent, two assistant superintendents, and a budget that staggered under the burden of two unnecessary salaries. This is a costly, wasteful process that has those who cannot teach or lead being placed in positions to make decisions and to devise requirements for those who can.


## <u>Board Members</u>

Believing that school boards are the highest authority within a school system, those studying school government ask hard questions of them.  It would be unfair, however, to blame school boards for all our problems.  There are many fine and dedicated Board Members!  I've watched their struggles and witnessed their sacrifices.  Unfortunately, there are also those who are mere figureheads to a powerful superintendent.  During interviews, I've found them to be quite candid.  Although some were bitter, what they told me matched what I experienced within the different systems where I've taught.

Some board members have run and served because they were sincerely motivated by the desire to help children.  Some have run and served because of the power and influence the office brought them.  Some have run strictly for personal gain. I talked with one board member who didn't know I was a teacher. "I just ran," he said, "to get the district's business for my agency." And he did get the business.  (Unfortunately, so did the district.)

Still others have run so they could correct an intolerable situation.  Once elected, however, they can lose their original purpose and courage as a result of the flattery, attention, and wheedling of the superintendent.

In one state, a teacher told me how a local businessman went to an open board meeting to see what was going on.  He said he was disgusted with the actions of the superintendent, and he was going to run for the board "to correct things."  He did run.  Soon after being elected, he was instrumental in giving this same superintendent a four-year contract—early.  This contract had to be bought out later, which made the district obligated to pay two superintendents' salaries for two years.

Board members play an important and sometimes difficult role.  Their responsibility is to set policy and to oversee the fiscal management of their district.  In so doing, they must keep in mind that the money they are overseeing belongs to the children.  This means they must take a firm stance against anyone who would misuse it.  This in itself makes it a difficult job.


## <u>Superintendents</u>

By now you may be wondering how these things happen.  They happen, in part, because in today's school systems, superintendents have to be rather charismatic individuals.  A good portion of their time is spent charming board members into giving them what they want, charming certain parents into believing that their children will turn out all right in the end, and charming overburdened property owners into agreeing to pass yet one more tax increase for themselves.  Sometimes, superintendents can charm everyone in the district into believing that what they are doing is best for the children, even when what they are actually doing is best for themselves.

Whereas there are many fine and dedicated superintendents, there are also the powerful, the corrupt, the greedy, and the incompetent. You will know which is which by their actions.

Some superintendents refuse to allow board meetings to be televised.  Some present their new contract early when new members join the board.  New members will often vote for it, because they don't yet understand how this superintendent operates.  Some superintendents hold informal meetings with their school boards to present ideas they don't want the public to know about.  If the board agrees to their request, it will pass with no opposition at the open board meeting.  If the board disagrees, the public will never know the nature of some of the requests made by the superintendents.

Some superintendents are also quite successful in circumventing accountability.  Under their orders, supervisors, personnel directors, or assistant superintendents tell principals and teachers what to do.  If anything goes awry, it is the fault of the principal or the teacher. Not only are the superintendents blameless, but any culpability lies two levels away from them. This is one way superintendents build a following that will be grateful enough to vote their way for a tax levy or for their choice of board members. There's another way they avoid accountability. Some superintendents maintain that since board members are not educators, they are unable to evaluate superintendents. The gentleman who shared this with me said, "And when you're a brand new board member in your first board meeting, wanting to make a difference, yet not wanting to be seen as a troublemaker right off, you fall for this."

Some superintendents grasp every financial advantage, taking moneys that should be benefiting the children, as they negotiate unbelievable contracts to seize all they can, even from bankrupt districts where children sit in deplorable conditions under crumbling ceilings or play on unsafe playground equipment. These exorbitant salaries do not tell the whole story, however. Depending on the district, for example, the salary figures that are published may not include the special medical benefits, paid-up life insurance policies, cars, expense accounts, car phones, retirement annuities, and sometimes even a membership at the area country club, not to mention the decadent buy-outs.


### **Have They Earned It?**

The following was recently reported:

> "New math. Superintendent's C-minus results
> win him an A-plus raise in salary. . . ."[2]

Thus, even though some administrators don't know how to fix the system, even though they don't have the incredible wisdom worthy of commanding such incredible remuneration, they are being given phenomenal financial rewards. I have been told many times, "Oh, yes, but such things happen everywhere, in any profession or business." That may be true, but what does that have to do with the most important and vital thing humankind does—educate their young?

It is time for our democratic, enlightened society to question why school superintendents and administrators should become a privileged group at the expense of the taxpayer—not to mention the children.

By permission of Mike Luckovich and Creators Syndicate.    3

## <u>Power to the Unqualified</u>

Wherever I have taught, observed classrooms, or interviewed teachers, I have found that my fellow teachers agree that one of the most crippling practices a teacher endures and children suffer under is that of placing administrators in positions that require judgments they are not qualified to make.  This happens in several ways.

It happens when the administrators are untrained in the area they are supervising or for which they are making decisions. It happens when those rooted more in business than in education place children where their presence will bring the district the most government funding rather than where they will receive appropriate help. One teacher of handicapped children told me how, in such cases, teachers are brushed aside and parents who try to fight it wind up with nothing but large legal fees.

One personnel director (in a district overrun with administrators), against the advice of teachers, often misplaced learning-disabled, handicapped, or remedial students. One of his decisions was to keep a five-year-old hearing-impaired child in our district rather than sending her to a special school because sending her elsewhere meant an extra cost to the district. The outcome for this little girl was tragic. She became disoriented and frightened in large school assemblies, but she was never placed where she could get the help she needed. In this way, the child's nightmare becomes the teacher's workplace.


## Run That By Me Again

Some administrators use educational jargon—those technical terms that cow the public. Parents say to themselves, "Here is this high-ranking educator talking; what do I know?" While some do know, not every administrator is fully qualified to use terms such as "attention deficit, hyperactivity, or underachiever," which are terms that describe real and viable disorders and should not be used loosely.

Often, by the time parents realize that the administrator was not fully qualified to use a particular technical term and that it was therefore not applicable to their child, this child is in junior high school and running from two to four years behind grade level. One mother said, "My son is in his second year of the same grade level in junior high school and can't do the work. He has slipped through the system because I listened to the administrators. Through the years, I was told that my son was an underachiever, and then that he was hyperactive, and lately, that he has an attention deficit." Unable to refute the language, she let the administrators handle the situation.


## Ego or Fear?

Some principals feel compelled to handle any situation calmly on their own, even bomb threats. In a few cases, this may be ego. Sometimes, however, the principals "had better" handle it because their superintendents want no problems in their school district that might prove either embarrassing or newsworthy. Nevertheless, this can affect the children.

A principal with whom I worked tried never to bother the superintendent with any problem whatsoever. When a little boy's nose began to bleed during a math lesson in my room, he told me he had stuck his eraser up his nose. By the time I looked, the eraser was out of sight. I hurried him to the office and asked for medical help. But the principal turned toward his office, saying, "I'll get my long-nosed tweezers."

I followed him out of the child's hearing. "The eraser could drop back into the child's throat," I said, "even into his windpipe or lung. I am requesting professional medical help." He brushed me aside and said, "You worry too much."

Outside of wrestling him to the ground (which I seriously considered) there was nothing left to do but comfort the child. The principal probed through the blood and tears. It seemed to take forever. Finally, he captured the eraser and announced triumphantly that he could handle these things.

But he was shaken. I could tell by his nervous question as I guided the child toward the door: "Mrs. Simpson, what were you doing anyway?"

I was shaken, too. I realized just how much by my answer (which was uncharacteristic). "Math. We were doing math, Mr. ______. I was showing him how one eraser minus one eraser equals zero."

## There's a Whole Lot of Guessin' Going On

Some administrators honestly don't know what to do for primary children even though they are educators.  Many have secondary backgrounds or were athletic coaches or have business backgrounds. Many were never trained for kindergarten or first or second grades.

Whereas they may be excellent in the area for which they were trained, how can we expect them to institute the correct measures for primary levels if they don't fully understand what those measures should be?  I know of no other field in which so many in charge have never worked in the trenches and will not accept the experiential advice of those who have.

An article in the Invester's Business Daily speaks to this.

> "Where are Edu-fads hatched?  Whole Language, other tracts brewed in Fed. Labs.  Part of the Education Department's Office of Educational and Research and Improvement,  OERI is a deceptively influential arm of the department.  It's source for much of the research that's powered recent curriculum changes in America's public schools.

> "Their cost?  About one-quarter of OERI's \$400 million annual budget.  Of course, education research and development makes up only a fraction of the \$30 billion in Federal education spending.

> "To foes, the labs have fostered some of the worst fads in American schools, from new math to whole language—which has replaced phonics as the way to teach kids reading in many schools."[4]

\$30 billion! \$400 million! \$100 million! The question is: How many teachers for smaller classes could we hire for these amounts? Not only that, we'd still be teaching phonics.

One idea fostered in labs is using only the Whole Language Approach to teach reading.  It is my belief and the belief of every teacher I've interviewed that, used alone and wrongly, this approach has produced an unfortunate number of nonreaders. I spoke with Dr. Jeanne S. Chall, Professor of Education, Emeritus, and former Director of the Reading Laboratory at the Graduate School of Education, Harvard University for 33 years. She explained the whole language theory in an interview.

> She said, "Starting in the late 70's the 'whole language' swept into American schools. Whole language theory encourages students to learn to read by relying mainly on their knowledge of language. It assumes that beginners will learn to sound out words from a knowledge of language. This is not confirmed by the existing research evidence."[5]

The Investor's Business Daily reported:

> "Programs backed by the labs include whole language, new math, outcome based education, developmentally appropriate learning and nondirective learning.

> "The idea behind whole language is that children will learn to read the same way they learn to speak— by learning the words in context. Memorizing words by flash cards is ditched. So is correct spelling. 'Creative spelling' is accepted instead."

The article concluded with the outcome for one state that:

> ". . . embraced whole language reading more than a decade ago. . . but in '94, state educators got a rude awakening. This state tied for last in reading achievement on the National Assessment of Educational Progress."[6]

In an interview one teacher shared this.  "I am a substitute teacher at the present time, and I want to tell you about this whole language approach that my district has adopted.  I subbed for this excellent teacher last year, and all but four of her children were reading. This year I subbed for her and only four of her children were reading. I asked her why.  Her answer—'This year I am being evaluated for tenure by my supervisors, and I dare not teach anything but the Whole Language Approach which this school district supports wholeheartedly.  In past years I taught a lot of phonics on the sly. Next year, after I get my tenure, I'll go back to my phonics instruction.  I just have to be very careful, especially when my supervisor is due.'"

This is one of the tragedies of education. In those districts where teachers are forced to obey the supervisors who are wrong, and where  the whole language approach to reading is used incorrectly, (as a reading method which deletes phonics rather than a reading philosophy which includes phonics), many children don't read.  I just spoke with one mother who is angry with her school district. She said, "I hate the fact that they don't teach phonics anymore. When my little boy brought his reading book home and called the word 'house' in one sentence a 'brick,' I asked if his teacher had corrected him.  He said, 'No, we're allowed to guess.'  I knew at this point I had to do something, so I began to teach him phonics at home."

We can see from this how lost our children are without phonics. This is particularly horrifying when we see how different are the beginning sounds of "house" and "brick."  What kind of reader would this child have been without his mother's help?

This brings up an interesting point.  When teachers who know how imperative phonics instruction is to the reading process are employed by such districts and teach phonics "on the sly" (as I certainly did), and when parents teach phonics at home, how accurate then are the evaluations of nonphonetic approaches? From my point of view, the equation seems to be: We're spending billions of dollars to produce wrong solutions to put us 20 years behind in learning.

The newest idea of possible solutions making the rounds is Whole Math. Somewhat akin to Whole Language, children develop their own methods of multiplying and dividing and learn that answers close to being correct are good enough.

In some states, until the 1970's, the responsibility of State Board Members consisted primarily of deciding such matters as how high the drinking fountains must be or determining other measurements of the physical plant. Then the Board members decided to become involved in the curriculum. Are they educators? In some states the rule is they must be lay people. If they are educators, they must not be currently working in the field of education.

Designing a program for young children that will work requires the insight of at least one person who has taught in the highly specialized field of the primary grade levels. This is the key forgotten element. Compare the situation with the medical field. Dermatologists are indeed highly respected and vital members of the medical profession. But would you want them to perform open-heart surgery on you?

Adept at blending into the system that spawns them, some administrators keep their lucrative positions even when they realize they don't really know the best way to proceed, even when they see the rates of failure and illiteracy, even when they see that children are not learning. "What has that got to do with my $10,000,000 salary?"

*      *      *

So! However our educational system got this bad, it remains that way partly because education has been taken out
of the hands of good teachers and principals and been placed elsewhere.

Picture this. We appoint a business person as chief of surgery at a major hospital. Just as a superintendent of schools who has never taught at the primary level can say, "We need to inspire children, we need to hire good teachers, and we need to keep the schools in good repair," the business person can say, "We need to keep the surgery spotlessly clean and sterile, we must keep the right equipment in good working order, and we must put the welfare of the patients first."

BUT, the question is—during the operation, shouldn't there be at least one surgeon in the room?

## 1) <u>Set policy only over areas for which you are trained.</u>

Those not trained in primary elementary education should not set policy for primary elementary education without the assistance of a primary educator. Although unrecognized as such, primary elementary education is a specialized field. As such it requires that someone who understands exactly how young children develop and learn set the policies, make the decisions on placement of the children, design the curriculum, and set subject priorities and time allotments. The time allotments must be fluid in early grades.

When Federal, state, or local officials say it is their right to set educational policy, they are wrong. It is never the right of anyone to set policy for areas in which they are untrained, or at least, not without the help of those who are.

The needs of children differ from school system to school system. Therefore, the local primary teachers and principals must set the policies for their districts rather than state officials, who are not only unqualified to do this by virtue of being lay people, but are many miles removed from the districts for which they are making the decisions. This one size-fits-all policy is nowhere more inappropriate than in the education of young children.

## 2) <u>Do not judge excellence by difficulty.</u>

The excellence of a school system will no longer be determined by the difficulty of the curriculum and how early children are forced to perform its tasks. The excellence of a school system will be determined by how well children are learning and FARING within it.

School administrators will tell you how proud they are of their school systems. When I probed more deeply and asked about the children who were unable to fit into this "advanced" system, I received many answers. For example, "Yes, that is a problem, but

we're known as a top-notch school district and we're proud of that."
Or, "But parents want it this way."

They never would answer my question directly.  This is
something to look for in searching out problems and finding
solutions.  Can the administrators answer hard questions about the
children?  NOT questions about the school system, the buildings
and grounds, the curriculum and how difficult it is, how parents
feel about the system, their rating among all other districts, the
salary schedule for teachers, or the amount of technical equipment
they have in the classroom—WHAT ABOUT THE CHILDREN?


3)  <u>**Don't give someone a high office just because they "want"
it.**</u>

Sometimes people who just "want" the position of power are
poorly trained for the position.  Or sometimes a "buddy system"
attitude places unqualified friends where they do not belong;
therefore, everyone involved suffers.

It has been said:

> "The only people who can be trusted with power
> are those who do not covet it."
>
> — Socrates

All leaders and administrators must own up to some sort of
honest appraisal concerning their qualifications for a certain
position. We can't expect that?  Then a citizens' group should
provide this service. Which brings us to the next solution.


4)  <u>**Form a group of knowledgeable persons.**</u>

A group of citizens—which should include, among others, an
accountant; an attorney; a primary, an intermediate, and a high-
school teacher; a minister; a business person; a banker and a
pediatrician—will demand access to position descriptions for each
administrator and the financial records.

It is time for the ones doing the paying to see what they are paying for. All administrators must explain their positions to this citizens' group and present a worksheet time schedule of what they do and how long it takes them. Full explanations are required. (Perhaps they could fill out cards similar to those teachers must fill out to denote the exact minutes spent on each subject.) In many districts, a comparison of these data will show many duplications of function; invented busywork; and the portion of time (as observed by teachers) spent in teachers' lounges, cafeterias, restaurants, and fun talk sessions among themselves.

It will also show that an amazing amount of their "work" could be done by good secretaries—a much overlooked, under-appreciated position, and a tremendous money-saving aid to school systems. In most districts where I've worked, the administrative staff could have been cut. The key factor to remember is that superintendents gain their status, prestige and salary to some measure by the number of administrators they command.

This committee of knowledgeable citizens can be a short-term group, but it will not be able to function without good teachers who know where the waste occurs. These teachers must be honest, incorruptible, and in a position of some security.

Without teachers this process may not work as well. In one city a citizens' group looked for and found many unnecessary positions. They did a masterful job. Unfortunately, they did not go deeply enough perhaps because they did not fully understand the workings of a school district. Teachers can tell you where the waste occurs.

Also, this is a more necessary place for parents to find themselves—in the financial records and the administrative offices, rather than in the classroom. This is not to say that parents may not act if they have an incompetent teacher. What they must stop doing is interfering with good teachers on matters of teaching procedures, placement of children, and especially on matters of discipline.

5) __Remove the layers in the system.__

With the information from the citizens' group in hand, every unnecessary position should be eliminated.  It may be possible to combine some positions.  After we have removed all the unnecessary personnel in the local systems, we can then do so in the state systems and finally in the federal system.  When all the waste is removed, this will simultaneously provide relief for the taxpayer, the children, and teachers.  The teachers and principals trained in elementary levels will be happy to set the guidelines for their particular district.  They are, of course, accountable by the same standards that now exist.

As the layers are removed, simplicity is the rule.  The concept to keep in mind is this—what are the only two segments of a school that we could not do without?  The answer is, the children and the teachers.  All others are extras.  We must scrutinize every administrator's position and ask the following:  Is this job absolutely necessary?  Is it being duplicated elsewhere?   Can it be done by someone else for a lot less money?

6) __Institute a control/auditing board to limit administrators' salaries and perks.__

The thing to remember here is that educational funds are the children's money, and even though some children sit in deplorable conditions, they cannot speak for themselves.  Someone with their interests at heart must speak for them.

7) __Abolish the law regarding reassignment.__

If an administrator, teacher, or principal is unfit to be an administrator, teacher, or principal, they are certainly unfit to supervise other administrators, teachers, or principals.  If they are doing a poor job in their position,  being dismissed is a more appropriate action than being rewarded.

## 8) **A superintendent must be made accountable.**

In addition to the school board, which may also be made up of noneducators, the superintendents must be made accountable to some degree to the teachers who will work closely with the school board in the evaluation process. Good superintendents listen to those qualified to speak for the children regarding educational needs—good teachers.


## 9) **Put reading first in primary grades.**

In the primary grades, let teachers decide time schedules according to the needs of their children. The rule is: First we learn to read and then we read to learn. Along with individual need and readiness, this is another absolute we have forgotten with children.


## 10) **First, last, foremost, and always—teach phonics!**

To teach children to read well so they will be avid readers for the rest of their lives, any approach to reading must include phonics. An approach based on guessing, substitution, or memorization, etc. will not give the children a firm base for attacking and decoding the many new words they will encounter throughout their lifetime.


## **Some Final Thoughts**

With an eye toward the total welfare of children we must remove layers in all education departments to obtain the money for smaller classes and simultaneously lower taxes for all citizens. The thing to remember here is: Not only are many of these unnecessary administrators absorbing far too much of the children's moneys while making decisions they are unqualified to make, but they are (in some situations) also doing a great deal of damage to the children in the process. It is now time to take you inside the classroom and show you some of the ways this damage occurs and how it affects the children.

Which brings us to supervisors!

# Chapter 4

Supervisors:  Expensive in More Ways Than One


"It is true that in the historic struggle between ignorance and knowledge, ignorance wins the battles, while knowledge wins the wars—but what if the battles are so decisive and debilitating that it takes generations or even centuries for the forces of knowledge to recuperate?"[1]

— Sydney J. Harris


Our educational system is winning neither battle nor war.  What is worse, the debilitation is further compounded by detrimental solutions instituted by those in leadership roles.  As explained in

Chapter 3, this is happening because those who do not fully understand how the very young learn have come up with solutions that prove more damaging to the children and teachers than did the original problem.

Those who try to fix our educational dilemmas remind us of the foxhounds a man was training for the big hunt. Things were not going well because the hounds were an excitable lot. The big day finally arrived, however, and as the hunt got under way the hounds got so excited while following the scent that they ran right on past the fox, thereby setting up the absurd picture of the fox chasing the hounds.[2]

Similarly, those chasing the answers to educational dilemmas, in many cases with self-interests hovering overhead, have run right on past the simpler prerequisites of all learning. The solutions they offer have distanced us even more from where we need to be.


## **The Look, Try, Discard, and Move On System**

In searching for educational solutions, those in power have tended to look at one area of education at a time and to try to fix that area, albeit inappropriately. When the situation doesn't change for the better, and despite the fact that the area has not been corrected, those in power discard that particular effort and move on to the next trendy issue.

For example, for a time teachers were looked upon as the sole reason for our educational dilemmas. Suggestions for change came at us from every quarter. The following are but a few of the ideas offered:

- We should send teachers back to school.
- Teachers should get their Master's Degrees
- Teachers should go to school longer.
- More accurate methods should be devised to measure their expertise.
- We should toughen certification.
- We should do yearly testing of teachers.

- We should give teachers incentive raises.
- Teachers should write more in their plan books.
- Time restrictions must be imposed on a teacher's school day.
- Time requirements must be devised for each subject, down to the minute.

At one point, it was suggested that paying a teacher $125 per student over the recommended class size might make them better teachers. Whereas it's nice to be rewarded for harder work, money could hardly help teachers in the classroom. They would still have far too many children with different needs to be met to provide for each of them at a level of optimum learning.


## <u>Now We Have the Answer—Supervisors!</u>

When it was decided that teachers needed help (and in some cases monitoring), supervisors became the answer. Today, some districts have supervisors, some do not, and some districts have supervisors whose role has evolved into something quite different than what was intended.

In one district, I worked closely with a teacher who was treated unfairly and she spoke to her principal, and then the superintendent. The issue was serious enough that, when nothing was done about it, she threatened to take it farther, past the superintendent, to the school board. The morning after the threat the supervisor was in her room. The supervisor stayed longer than usual and wrote a damaging evaluation. On the strength of this evaluation, the teacher was asked to resign. She refused. The supervisor returned again and again until the unnerved teacher, watching her permanent file being filled with damaging evaluations, and with an eye toward future employment, finally resigned.

In some districts some supervisors can drift into the position of informer if the superintendent is so inclined. After the board meeting where this was the case and a teacher was being fired, I spoke to one of the parents, who was a university professor of education. He explained that this is becoming an accepted practice because school districts are in such dire straits that some superintendents contend they need every possible edge. Accepted practice or not, it did happen and I had several opportunities to watch the process.

Although I'm certain that some supervisors are good and well-intentioned, throughout my years of teaching and my research for this book, I never found a teacher who could commend this concept. In some cases it was not because they disliked their supervisors per se. It was, perhaps, because the very nature of the position causes it to be regarded as still another source of stress and pressure among the many already facing the teacher. One teacher put it this way: "I feel so helpless. I'm frustrated because I know what's right and what works for my class, but they tie my hands." In any case, taxpayers can't afford good supervisors monetarily, and they can't afford bad ones monetarily or educationally.


**<u>The Trickle-Down Theory</u>**

Eventually, such situations began to affect the children we were teaching—partially because of the teacher's distressed state of mind, but from more than that. In writing this book I have found it difficult to separate what happens to the teacher from what happens to the children. The two are linked inseparably by the bond of mutual helplessness—what was wrongly required of the teacher affected the children, and what was wrongly required of the children affected the teacher. Under the current system, both are treated as nonentities. Each is set upon from all sides by the whims of a hierarchy that hasn't a clue as to what either children or teachers are about.

It is time for parents to see how the idea of supervisors has gone awry in some districts. This has not only affected the teachers, but inevitably the children as well. And, taxpayers, perhaps you would like to see what some of your tax money is buying. The rest of this chapter takes you inside the classroom to show you just that.

<u>**"Our Pet Bugaboos"**</u>

In one district, supervisors presented their new ideas, which they termed "our pet bugaboos," to us in meetings that often left good teachers distressed and depressed. One of the more damaging bugaboos came the year they locked the teachers' book cabinets, which were located in the hallways. These cabinets were filled with past reading books of all levels, and the teachers used them to reinforce what children were learning in their current reading program.

Teachers used these books as extra reading materials for all students, but especially for the more advanced children. We also used them for afternoon reading groups, during which time children could pick the story they wanted to read next. This gave them a freedom that the regular series could not, which made them feel important. They delighted in the fact that they were now readers who could go outside their regular reading book and that what they had learned also applied here.

One year teachers got a new reading program that they did not like. Although it contained excellent phonics instruction, it did not provide enough practice reading material. At times the same story was used for several days, and that story would sometimes consist of the same sentence over and over with the addition of only one new word per line (and a picture was provided). Thus, the children were not watching or sounding out words, they were merely reciting the same sentence from memory.

Because of this, teachers taught this reading series and then turned to their cabinets for extra practice reading. But this year we found the cabinets were locked. Assuming this to be an oversight, I went to the office for the keys, where I learned it was no mistake. My principal referred me to a supervisor, who explained that because some of the teachers didn't like the new program, she was afraid they would not use it if the old books were available. Therefore, we would be required to use only the new program for the year.

I worked from the belief that the love of reading is as important as the mechanics and that each is crucial to the other. Therefore, I could not give up, and other teachers urged me on.

I again went to the supervisor, armed with what I felt to be irrefutable arguments.  I explained that her fears were groundless because a teacher could not teach from the other books and then switch to the new reading series whenever a supervisor walked in. Reading programs consist of progressive steps whereby skills learned in Chapters 1 through 5 are necessary to be able to do the work in  Chapter 6.  Therefore, I pointed out, it would be obvious if a teacher were not using the new series. The supervisor remained unmoved and responded, "Just try it, Norma.  Just call it my little pet bugaboo for this year."

The cabinets remained locked all year.  By the time the principal realized how much damage this "bugaboo" was creating, the damage to the children had already been done. The principal called me in and delivered a half-hearted apology.  "Well, I guess we were too hard on you all."  He still didn't get it.  The loss had been to the children.


## Another Repressive Bugaboo

A similar thing happened with arithmetic.  In this particular district, children learned Math Facts 1 through 10 in the first grade, and then reviewed those and learned 11 through 20 in the second grade.

Our absolute best tool for this was our timed Math Fact Tests. These tests provided the only means for children to see which facts they actually knew and which they needed to continue to study. Afterward, I would call them up to my desk individually and show them which combinations they still needed to work on and how much better they had done this week than the preceding week.  It was a good time because this was a place where the teacher could be positive no matter how far behind a child was.  Also, children thrive on this individual attention, which made them want to know more facts for the following week's tests.

Then, in our first supervisor's meeting of that school year, we were told, "No more timed Math Fact Tests." We assumed someone was misusing them.  We discussed with the supervisor how, unless children are timed, they could involuntarily be counting the facts out in their heads or on their fingers. As a result, they might think they knew them when they really didn't.

"Couldn't we continue to use the timed tests," we asked, "and have supervisors work with anyone who is abusing them?" When it became evident that there would be no more timed tests, one teacher asked in frustration, "Well, whose idea was this anyway, the State's, the district's, or yours?" Finally the supervisor admitted, "The math textbook salesman suggested it to me."

Unlike the locked book cabinets, this was a problem we could work around if we were willing to accept the consequences should a supervisor walk in during a test. Also, it was difficult to answer such questions as "Do you give timed math tests?" (asked by the parents) or "Is this a timed math fact test?" (asked by the children). "No. No, this is just a little exercise so that you can see how much more you need to study." Rather pitiful, I know. But my fellow teacher across the hall and I continued to use the math fact tests, our children continued to know the math facts, and we had added one more stressor to our workday.

We felt this was necessary because the potential damage involved more than the children's not knowing their math facts well enough. When these second-graders left our rooms for the third grade, they went directly into the study of the multiplication tables. The third-grade teachers explained that if children did not have their addition and subtraction facts firmly in mind, real confusion resulted. Some children could manage, but many could not.


## Some More of My Agendas for You Teachers.


In one district teachers were required to make up games for every subject they taught. In another district teachers were not allowed to repeat the child's response. Instead, the child would have to repeat the answer until every student could hear it. When this was required of a shy child, each repetition of an answer became softer rather than louder. When a supervisor was observing, shy children would glance back at him/her and become even shier. It is impossible to get an intelligible response under these circumstances. When we eventually would have to repeat a child's answer for the rest of the class, we could see the black magic marker (which some supervisors used) begin to move.

Some supervisors insisted that computers be used and then decided the amount of time teachers should spend on this instruction. In one school system, first-grade teachers were appalled at the amount of time this required computer work took from reading instruction. In interviews, however, in some districts, I found secondary teachers were equally appalled. Said one teacher, "We have one hour a day to teach our subject. My supervisor requires that I spend fifteen minutes of it on computers. It's too much."

In one school system, one of the most instructive fun things teachers did in second grade was a Pilgrim/Indian Day in November. We studied Pilgrims, and Indians, with the culminating activity being an actual day in the life of a Pilgrim boy and girl. Our lunch was a turkey dinner.

Our classroom was arranged just like the one-room schools were. There were no pencils or paper, and the children used chalk on the slates teachers made out of black and brown construction paper. The children were given instruction sheets on how to make costumes out of old clothes. Teachers also wore costumes. The teachers were grim, there was no laughing, and we had long switches that we tapped on the floor for attention. The children loved it.

The mothers brought the dinner for their children's classroom. They brought all the things the Pilgrims and Indians ate, including homemade bread. We, the teacher and children, made the butter for that bread. We put all the children's desks out in the long hallway arranging them into one long table. White paper was used as a tablecloth, and the room mothers and I served the children. In the afternoon, we pieced a quilt, which I later quilted. Need I say how much the children enjoyed this, or how much better they understood the life of Pilgrim children thereafter?

Then we received new social studies books in which the Pilgrim and Indian unit was the last chapter. We were told there would be no more Pilgrim/Indian/Feast Day because they would be inappropriate in May. We said this was no problem; we would do that unit in November instead. We were told to do that lesson in May, and no feast!

We offered to give up the dinner if we could just continue our Pilgrim one-room school day. This request was also denied.

One teacher I interviewed reminded me that she took up the fight when I left. They wrote letters, gathered petitions, and explained that it really made no difference which chapters were taught in which months as long as all were taught. The teachers were told to do the units as they appeared in the book. This is another example of the teachers being overruled by the arbitrary, personal preference of an administrator.


## Goodbye Plan Book, I Sure Miss You

A plan book is a book that teachers fill out each week. It contains all the lessons to be taught, with page numbers, workbook page numbers, and the seatwork for each subject. In one district, supervisors suddenly decided that teachers should write all the objectives for each subject in their plan book, even though these objectives were clearly written in the textbooks at the beginning of each lesson.

When the teachers explained that would leave no room for anything else, including page numbers for our substitute teachers, their answer showed how far out of touch supervisors can become after years out of the classroom. They said, "Well, the children know where they are." Depending on a first- or second-grader to tell a sub where they are in any subject or how far they are supposed to go for that day could only result in mass confusion. For example, if you ask six different children for the information, you could get six different answers. Also, this was busy work that took up a great deal of a teacher's time.

When I first began teaching, my plan book was my best teaching tool. Through the years, however, because of the supervisors' revisions, it became something of no use to me or to anyone else. In the end, it was merely a textbook of copied objectives that supervisors would glance at during their visits. All that work accomplished nothing except to waste a teacher's time.

In some states, they have "Distinguished Educators" rather than supervisors. One teacher told me that in his school district the Distinguished Educator collects their plan books periodically and grades them.

To our explanation that the plan book was for us and for substitute teachers, we were told, "If you don't like it, have two plan books." They had evidently forgotten (if they ever knew) how long it takes to do one plan book.


## This Is Another Fine Mess You've Gotten Us Into

In another district, the supervisors decided that the children should be doing reading seatwork the entire time the teacher was conducting reading groups. In the first and second grades, this accounted for a good portion of the day. Some of us had excellent seatwork that prepared the children in all phases of language. We also had fun math sheets that not only taught but were enjoyed, and funny poems for writing lessons, accompanied by art work to develop young imaginations.

Now we were being told to make up enough reading seatwork, (from just the previous day's reading lesson) that would last the entire time we were dealing with four or five reading groups. (An impossibility.) I asked if all seatwork could be considered reading since the children had to read to do it. I was told, "No." Then I asked if the language and spelling could be considered reading. Same answer. We later found that our supervisor had gotten this idea from the supervisor of intermediate grades, at which levels reading groups took much less time.

## **Caught!**

It was inevitable that I should get caught. My own discipline system worked well. It was successful because my children understood that if they obeyed the rules we had a fun day. They knew the reasons for the rules and that they were fair. They also knew I would follow through.

But to address the problems some teachers had with discipline, we all had to use the new system our supervisor had chosen. For the first offense, the child's name was written on the board as a warning. For the next offense, an "x" was written by the name, which meant five minutes of recess lost. When the name had three "x's" beside it, the child would miss the entire recess.

With this system, instead of knowing they could not misbehave at all, the children learned they could misbehave four times before missing recess. Also, the learning atmosphere was disrupted by calling attention to behavior so many times.

This was another practice that, in all good conscience, I could not follow. This time, however, my luck had run out. Actually, I had forgotten all about it. Worse, I did not remember it until a child did something deemed inappropriate by the watching supervisor, who then looked at me in challenge. I wrote the child's name on the board, who asked sweetly, innocently, and loudly, "Mrs. Simpson, what's my name doing there on that board?" And the magic marker began to move.


## **On Intricate Evaluation Systems and Centipedes**

Some supervisors would devise evaluation systems, each one more elaborate than the previous one. One of these systems had 26 broad headings with subcategories underneath. One section involved counting and recording each type of question we asked the children.

The number of times we said "okay" or "all right" were also recorded, as was the number of times we repeated, developed, rejected, or accepted the child's response. In addition, the supervisors counted the number of times we addressed student behavior and recorded how closely together these incidents occurred. They also counted the number of times we said "good," how many times we smiled, and the number of unused papers on a child's desk—among other things.

Seeing that marker moving across a sheet was unnerving. We felt like the centipede who was once asked how he was able to run with all those legs. According to the poem, as he began to consider which leg came after which, he wound up in a ditch. It was the same for teachers. Trying to consider each question before we asked it, trying to act natural for the children, trying not to say "okay" or "all right," trying never to repeat what a child said, and trying to remember all 26+ categories in front of a critical observer, and then trying to be a cheerful, effective teacher was—well, that centipede had nothing on us.

## There's More

If we asked some supervisors a question or for advice (which was supposed to be their reason for being), this could wind up on our evaluation sheet as a weakness that we needed to correct (as if they had discovered this defect in us all by themselves). Some of them joked about needing something to write on our sheets; their theory was that the more they could find to write about, the more it would appear they were needed.

Some supervisors also counted minutes. I was once written up (on Columbus Day) for spending 25 minutes on arithmetic rather than the required 40. It was true that the instructional part of the lesson lasted only 25 minutes, but the children then had two math workbook sheets that took about five minutes each to complete and a fun math sheet with blocks that they numbered to 100. By reading the instructions and correctly coloring certain blocks, the children produced the ship the Pinta. That actually put me a minute or two over the required 40, but the 25 went into my file.

In all fairness to supervisors, some of the requirements they impose are mandated by the state. Time allotment is one such requirement in some areas. But in all fairness to the State, a supervisor was not required to list the times inaccurately so as to find "trouble spots" in teachers or to justify their positions and large salaries.

Some supervisors plan social events and expect teachers to attend. I interviewed one group of teachers who told me their supervisor keeps inviting them to her home for parties. They said that some of them are very uncomfortable with this because of the way she treats them and because they have social lives of their own. When I asked them if they attended these functions, one teacher explained, "Yes, we attend. It's kind of a passive-aggressive thing, you know? I mean, it's not verbalized as such, but we all pretty much feel like we'd better go or else."

## Workshops

Another loss to teachers resulted from supervisors attending workshops that were designed for the teachers. When they returned from these workshops, they would present one or two ideas they insisted we try. Having no classes of their own to discover what worked and what didn't, we became their learning labs while having no say whatsoever.

I was permitted to attend only one workshop in 17 years. While there, I took down some 40 ideas, which I shared with the other teachers. Each of us could then use what suited our own personality or that of a particular class.

## How Cost Effective Are Supervisors?

In addition to everything else, having supervisors is an expensive practice. That Distinguished Educator you read about earlier makes $100,000 a year. Even if the supervisor is good, consider the cost for the one, sweet, unobtrusive supervisor I had in one district. He went about looking in doors saying, "I can see that learning is taking place. Carry on. If you need me, let me know." But incompetent teachers do not call attention to themselves by asking too many questions, and good teachers do not have time to deal with the bad ideas that come from someone who has not taught in a classroom in 20 years, if ever. The money is wasted.

When the purpose of supervisors is to oversee incompetent teachers, the cost is even greater. The system is not only leaving children in the care of incompetent teachers, but is spending millions of dollars to monitor that incompetency.

When supervisors move beyond the incompetency issue, the cost is indeterminable. When they begin distressing, disturbing, and crippling good teachers by tying their hands, the damage becomes threefold: 1) these salaries take large amounts of money that is needed elsewhere, 2) the children are being seriously damaged, and 3) we are losing our best teachers.

As is addressed in the next chapter, the supervisors' requirements make up only part of a teacher's workplace. Despite all this expenditure, however, nothing changed. The children's test scores continued to fall, they stopped looking at teachers as closely (which left unaddressed the incompetency problem in school), and moved on to another area. Only thing was—they left the supervisors!

*    *    *

By looking at one area, not really correcting anything and then moving on, we have run right on past our answers. In some districts, the use of supervisors, who help keep the battles between ignorance and knowledge decisive and debilitating, has left many of our children scarred for life. Life patterns are set early and can rarely be recaptured. If the children miss out on very much in one grade level, far too much material will be coming at them for them to recoup in the next level.

Parents have no way of knowing some of these things. How could they? Their comments to teachers make it quite apparent

96

what they don't know.  I received many suggestions from parents through the years, summed up by one father who said to me, "You teachers ought to be allowed to do your own thing. You know, use your imagination.  Creative freedom is what you need!"

Obviously, he'd never met a supervisor.

## 1) <u>Eliminate supervisors.  Return principals to this position.</u>

Even if some supervisors are good, principals are still the best evaluators of their teachers because they see them in all the situations they face regarding discipline, learning, control, and crises.  After the rush of the first days of school, a principal supervises and evaluates teachers.

I've visited schools where they do not have supervisors.  In some of these schools the principals know every teacher and if they are incompetent, they are gone.  If they are good, they are protected, supported, backed, encouraged and recognized as the backbone of the educational system.

Wherever supervisors also evaluate teachers, the public is paying for two supervisors.  School systems cannot afford this.  Tax-payers cannot afford this.  As you can see, we've just found a great deal of money that will provide more teachers for smaller classes.

## 2) <u>Choose a good lead teacher at each grade level.</u>

A good lead teacher at each grade level will help new teachers and be available for teachers who need some guidance.  This teacher's abilities will be far more current than those of the supervisors, many of whom have not taught in a classroom for some time.  This lead teacher will also be far more familiar with what actually works in today's classrooms.

Under no circumstances should lead teachers use evaluations sheets, or report to anyone regarding the teachers. The lead teacher is there for guidance and nothing more.  In this way, teachers will feel freer to consult this fellow teacher than an administrator. Even if the lead teacher is given a small increase in salary, it's minuscule compared with supervisors' salaries.

## 3) **If teachers need help, send *help*.**

If teachers need help, the use of a teacher's aide would be of much more value to the teacher and the children—for a fraction of the cost.


## 4) **Allow teachers to go to workshops.**

A teacher who attends a workshop can bring back all the ideas and distribute them among the other teachers, who can then pick and choose which ideas will work with their particular classes.


## 5) **Give teachers the freedom to be their own creative selves.**

In the same way we force all children into the same mold, some school districts have supervisors who force all teachers to be alike. In my years of experience, I've never had a principal ask me to do the silly things requested by some of my supervisors. I've had principals who told me to be my own creative self. "As long as the children are learning, do your own thing," they said. And before the advent of supervisors, we did just that and then shared our good ideas with one another.

We must never force all teachers to teach in the same way. And, we must NEVER, never allow anyone who believes in locking up book cabinets to remain employed by a school district.

# Chapter 5

Teachers:  The Good, the Bad, and the Beautiful


> It is only through love that one ever succeeds in teaching anyone anything.  Any other kind of teacher is merely an instructor.
>
> — Johann Heinrich Pestalozzi


Good teachers love their students.  They see each child as unique, and they want each one to be successful.  Unfortunately, not all teachers can be classified as "good," which makes it necessary to address the issue of  incompetency.  Addressing this issue is necessary because incompetency reaches far into the recesses of a school district and affects everyone.

## The Incompetent Teacher

> "The secret of education lies in respecting the pupil."
>
> — Ralph Waldo Emerson

There are many levels of incompetency. The worst scenario is the teacher who does not like children, much less love and respect them.

Teaching does not consist of the "over-under" relationship that many adults think it does—"I'm older, I'm smarter, I'm boss." Actually the teacher and child are equals. This equality should not be confused with teachers being more mature and trained so they can set the perimeters of discipline and learning; instead, it refers to being equal in personhood, worth, and rights. A child has the right to be respected.


## How Do They Get Hired, and How Do They Stay?


The questions most frequently raised regarding incompetency are, "How do incompetent teachers get hired?" and "How do they stay employed in a district?" There are several answers.

Sometimes the one doing the hiring is not the best judge of teacher competency. Too often the "hirer" has never taught or doesn't know enough about teaching methods and concepts to probe. During my interviews, I was never asked any questions that were deeply relevant to the educational process, partially because those doing the hiring didn't know what to ask.

Some administrators have their own personal selection system. For example, one superintendent told me, "I only hire beautiful teachers. In this way the children live in a lovely, wonderful place." Some superintendents refuse to hire teachers who have too many years of experience because they command higher salaries.

Some incompetent teachers are employed because they are "automatic hirables" (i.e., they are friends or relatives of administrators or board members), and they remain employed regardless of how incompetent they are or how incompetent they become. Some districts also have "pets," who flatter administrators and court their favor.


## Don't Touch Those Books

No amount of reasoning on the part of the teachers can intervene on the children's behalf, not even in the most extreme cases. For example, a librarian roped off the books, forbade children to touch them, and defended the practice with, "I'll hand them the books they choose. Handling wears out our books sooner." I argued vehemently that books should be our most expendable product and that children should be free to browse, touch, choose, and hold. Besides, in the limited time this librarian had with the children, she could not get around to all of them more than once, if that. My arguments, however, failed to impress this administrator's relative.


## Incompetence as Process

Incompetency can develop. Newer teachers may come to the system filled with enthusiasm and high ideals and have the potential of becoming good teachers. Then they become disturbed by some of the things they are required to do or by those things they are not allowed to do. Thus, they begin to "go along" with the system, and in time, they become incompetent. One teacher explained, "Look, I tried; but it's their ballpark and I have to play in it their way."

Some young new teachers have not had the proper training to be on their own in the classroom. One young teacher confided to me that she was at a loss and asked for my help. She said that during her student teaching she had a disagreement with her supervising teacher who punished the children by taking away their milk snack. (Talk about incompetency.) Because many of these children were poor, she asked if some other disciplinary measure could be found. The supervising teacher became furious that this student teacher would dare question her methods and refused to give her any further help or instruction.

Young teachers are often afraid to jeopardize their positions by asking for help.  (Note, this young teacher came to me rather than to her supervisor.)  As a result, the system becomes their teacher, and they are slowly and carefully taught to be incompetent.


## On Being a Pal

Many incompetent teachers do not understand discipline.  They often say, "I want my children to love me."  When they strive not to lose love, however, they can lose control.

Sometimes when teachers try to become the children's pal, they can gradually abdicate their positions of authority by making those tiny concessions and compromises necessary to maintain the "palship."  That children will not love their teachers if they make them obey is a fallacy.  Deep within, children need and cry out for loving discipline, and they love the teacher who provides it.

Discipline is the training that corrects problems and helps the children to develop self-discipline.  Incompetent teachers see discipline as punishment.  They do not explain to the children why good behavior is required or necessary.  They wouldn't agree that the phrase "because I say so" should be abolished from the English language.


## "I Need, I Want"

Incompetency also develops when teachers begin to think more of what they want than of the children's needs and then design their days accordingly.  Some teachers do not want to teach certain children.  They say they need "sparkplugs" (bright children) in their classes.  They want.  They need.  It is not the children's task to make teaching easier for the teacher; it is the teachers' task to make learning possible for the children.

Sometimes principals want to fire incompetent teachers, but cannot. This is the age of the lawsuit, and many times, for various reasons, principals cannot do what they know is right, even for the children. So these incompetent teachers stay on, and eventually, the inevitable happens—they become tenured. In time, no one can explain it. "Look, look," exclaims the principal, "How did this happen?"

"Yes, yes!" echoes the supervisor. "However did this happen?"


## **Incompetency Reaches Out**

You read in Chapter 4 how, in an effort to address the incompetency problem, some supervisors come up with outlandish systems to keep tabs on incompetent teachers. To utilize those systems, they then insist that all teachers do the same things. Although the actions they insist upon might be one step above those that incompetent teachers are taking, they are still light years behind the methods of good teachers. Like water, then, incompetency descends to its own level, taking everyone along with it. Like the children, teachers are required to do the same thing as everyone else. This forces good teachers to become as incompetent as their incompetent counterparts—in deed if not in spirit.

To use my own experience as an example, I had developed language seatwork with which my supervisor was pleased. More important, the teachers who got my children in the next grade level could tell how effective it was. Two years later, however, because some teachers had developed inadequate seatwork, we were all supposed to begin using the supervisor's method. This new method was so inferior to mine that I continued with my own seatwork at the risk of being caught by my supervisor. To hide what I was doing, I was forced to copy all the work on ditto stencils and run off copies rather than writing the work on the blackboard where the supervisor could readily see it. This wasted valuable time and paper, besides creating a filing and storage problem.

Whereas forcing all teachers to do the same things at the same time actually does nothing for the incompetent teacher, it discourages and distresses good teachers and makes their workday very stressful.  No, we can't do our own thing and then change to a supervisor's method when they arrive at our door.  We don't always know when they're going to observe us, and we can't use one method one day and change to another the moment the supervisor arrives.  For one thing, not only do children have an unerring ability to spot chicanery; they feel it is their primary, sole, and essential duty to call it to everyone's attention.  "But what does this mean, Mrs. Simpson?"  Or worse—"But we've never done this before."


## Punishment as Reward

Good teachers are punished by the very nature of incompetency.  For example, in some districts good teachers have to endure stacked classes like those discussed in Chapter Two.  Good teachers with stacked classes are reminded periodically that the number of students retained in their classes reflects on their teaching skills.  Consideration is not always given to the considerable number of "special" children in their classes compared with their incompetent counterparts who have few or none.

I once asked a principal who was a good friend if he stacked the classes of his best teachers.  He studied the carpet for a few moments and then nodded his head.  "We get as many good years out of teachers as we can . . . for the children's sakes."

The nature of incompetency can keep a good teacher at a certain grade level permanently.  Sometimes good teachers ask for a grade level change; however, if they are needed in the  level where they are, they are not moved.  Request after request may be ignored, even if the teacher making the request has seniority.  Depending on their stamina, this can shorten the career of good teachers.


## The Absolute Bottom Rung

Where I have worked, teachers lived in an aura and atmosphere commensurate with being on the absolute bottom rung of the educational ladder. The maze-like obstacle course they must run seems to have been deliberately designed to test their patience and endurance. Many of the things they are required to do are degrading. Taken individually, they may sound trivial; but when combined with all you've read in the first three chapters, you will have a better understanding of where a teacher "lives." The following are just a few examples.

In some districts, teachers must sign in and out, supposedly so the administrators will know when a teacher is in the building. Sometimes, after the children are gone, a teacher may need to leave the building a few minutes early for a personal meeting or a doctor's appointment. When they arrive in the office to sign out early, however, they are questioned and reminded of the professionalism that keeps teachers in their rooms long after the children have departed. This attitude prevails even though the administrators know how much work teachers do at home each night.

In some districts, teachers cannot ask a custodian for anything. They must fill out a form and wait. This can sometimes be difficult; e.g., when a furnace goes out in subzero weather or a child throws up. The custodian might be in the hallway right outside the classroom door, but teachers still have to go through the principal for custodial services. When a child was sick in my room, I asked the custodian to help me because, although I knew the rule, I didn't understand (or couldn't believe) that it applied to emergencies. The custodian helped me, but later an administrator reminded me, "Next time, fill out a form."

In some districts, principals or supervisors go through the teachers' desk drawers, cupboards, and closets. One teacher had saved some very old readers as keepsakes. Over the summer, the principal cleaned out her closet and threw them away. His comment was, "They're too old to be used." On one occasion I returned to my room to find a supervisor rifling through my desk drawers. When questioned, she explained that everything in that district belonged to the district, even my desk.

Sometimes "favorite" teachers are given authority over supplies because too many supplies are being used for the budget. Their efforts to make an even greater impression on the administrators who put them in charge can result in teachers having to explain and justify their needs to fellow teachers. For example, "But we do this much seatwork a day, so I need this much paper." Or, "Yes, I do sharpen all the children's pencils myself to make them last longer." Or, "Yes, I did put the lids back on the paste jars; we just used more this quarter."

## **Teacher Influence Among Other Personnel**

In many districts, the classroom teacher has the lowest status among all the school personnel. Although there are many fine people in all the positions I discuss in this book, there are also those who are not so fine. For example, in one school system I requested that one of my children be tested by the school psychologist. I explained that something was disturbing her and that, in my opinion, her performance was not indicative of her ability. I showed the psychologist her drawings, which had alarmed me. When all else failed, I made the subjective observation, "Well, just look in her eyes; you can see she's troubled." She laughed. When I persisted she finally reminded me, "But you're not a psychologist."

After the psychologist tested the child, we met with the parents. She told them that their child was a perfectly happy little girl who fell on the high side of the normal range of intelligence. The parents, who had heretofore been complimentary and grateful, turned to me angrily and demanded, "Well, if she's normal and happy, then why isn't she learning? What are you doing to help her?" An ugly scene followed, and they refused to work with me any further, which punished the child.

The following year a teacher who had this child at the next grade level asked me, "How come you never had this girl tested, or did she just get this bad over the summer?" I told her she had been tested. The teacher said there was no evidence of that anywhere. When I asked her what she meant by "this bad," she explained the child was now in intensive psychotherapy.

I went in search of all the papers I had placed in the appropriate files. I had been particularly careful to record everything because I had disagreed with the psychologist's findings. Everything was gone. Even the permanent record card on which I and other teachers had recorded tests results was missing. In its place was a new, blank card. In short, there was no record whatsoever that this child had ever been psychologically tested.

One young girl told her story after she graduated. While in school, she had tried to tell her story through her drawings. She was being abused by her father but she said, no one caught it. Maybe and maybe not. Many times other teachers and I have reported what we felt were significant signs of abuse in children, only to be told one of four things: "There's nothing we can do; you worry too much; we can be sued; don't get involved."

Also, some nurses would not take our input about a child. For example, a little girl who never complained told me she was going to throw up. I sent her to the health room. She returned moments later and said she couldn't go home because she didn't have a fever. This round trip to the health room was repeated twice more before I asked the teacher across the hall to watch my class so I could take her to the health room myself. I asked the nurse to send her home.

I explained to a stonily silent nurse that I knew this child and that I myself had been ill many times with no elevated temperature. I called attention to the child's history of honesty, her color, her eyes, and her obvious weakness. Silence. Finally, I asked if the child could at least lie down while I took my class to lunch. Now she spoke. "Say, that's probably what she needs, something in her stomach." After lunch, this child threw up several times throughout the classroom, but she was never allowed to go home.

This is another example of the rules being made for adults rather than for children. Teachers are not complaining about the rules a nurse must make, we understand those. All we ask is to have some input because we know our children better than anyone else in the school district.

This lack of influence is also apparent wherever teachers have little if any say about their benefit packages, their evaluations, their working conditions, textbook selections, the grade level they teach, or on the placement of their students. We are not asking to dominate, just to contribute.


## <u>Fear as Companion</u>

Teachers can work in fear resulting from many sources. In some districts, they dread the supervisors' visits. Given the unpredictability of 32 children, teaching in front of observers is difficult.

A principal and a State Education official visited the classroom of one of my friends. Following what she thought was a good lesson, she called for questions. Delighted at the raised hands (which denoted interest), she called on a boy who asked, "Are those your real teeth?" If you were liked, such an incident was considered cute. If you were not, it was considered indicative of poor teaching.

In another district, a teacher was known for three things—being an excellent teacher, being religious, and never swearing. One morning when I arrived at school I found her red-faced and rushing about. When I asked her what was wrong, she cried out, "Oh, the damn supervisor's coming!" That incident gave me a pretty good picture of how I looked when it was my turn to be observed by a supervisor.

Because of the verbal assaults they receive, some teachers are afraid of their students. They also fear belligerent parents and the guns, grenades, and other weapons that are finding their way into the classroom.

Teachers also fear what an angry parent might tell an administrator about them. For example, one parent stormed to the principal's office to report me because I would not place her child in a more advanced reading group. She was going to have her son moved to another room. She said this in front of all my other parents (it was Open House) and all along the hallways on her way to the office. She was successful in getting the principal to agree to remove the child. Before this move could be made, however, she asked other parents about me. What they told her sent her back into my room after school the following day.  She apologized, and asked me to keep her son.  As she left my room,  she walked down a hallway into a group of waiting parents (and a teacher whom she didn't see) and said, "Well, I guess I got her told."

Another fear concerns what children may tell their parents after teachers have disciplined them.  One furious parent came to school to report me because her daughter had told her, "This girl pushed me and Mrs. Simpson punished me."  This was true; however, her daughter had failed to mention that she had bitten the little girl, who then pushed her away.  In the stories they take home, young children can be great "leaver-outers."

Another fear teachers live with is that they will not be backed by administrators.  In some districts they are; in others they are not.  In still others, teachers are assured they will be backed; but when situations arise that call for such backing, they do not receive it.  If teachers hold firm or speak out, they can be moved to the least desirable  school in the district or be dismissed.


## Let Me Entertain You

Good teachers realize the importance of their profession—they are responsible for the education of our nation's children.  Yet they work under some of the most debilitating stresses of any profession.

Some of the stress results from the very nature of their responsibility for the well-being, education, and safety of some 30 children a year.  Much of the stress a teacher endures, however, is totally unnecessary.  For example, a more recent method of school reform has as one of its precepts—if students fail/teachers are fired.  Nothing could be more debilitating or unfair to teachers in light of the countless variables that determine whether a child can or cannot proceed to the next grade level.  Instead of providing the teacher with all the support and help that is humanly possible to give, the agenda seems to be to add all the stress it is humanly possible to produce.

Some districts provide more support and cause less stress than others.  There might even be some perfect school districts somewhere, although I have never worked in one nor interviewed a teacher who had.

In addition to all the other things you now know about teachers, they're on stage seven hours a day. They try to maintain a positive outlook in the face of fear, stress, pressure, and silly rules. They attempt to function as a human computer that remembers the abilities, disabilities, learning styles, problem areas, personality traits, and sensitivities of each student, as well as the personality traits and quirks of their parents and the supervisors. At the same time, they strive to be more interesting than television.

Good teachers also understand this: Children need to know that in school (if no place else), there is one person who cares and wants them to succeed and become all they can be. When a child loves the teacher and the teacher loves the child, this provides the most fertile ground for learning. If children have a great home life, all the better. Many do not.

## <u>What We're Doing to Our Good Teachers</u>

In desperation, education officials keep mandating more and more requirements but getting less and less results. Therein, another vicious circle emerges. Children need creative teachers. School officials mandate into oblivion that creativity. Many creative teachers leave the profession. Many creative persons refuse to enter the profession. Children lose creative teachers.

We lose far too many good teachers when we tie their hands, restrict their activities, mandate their every move, smother their vivacity, regiment their schedules, kill their spirits, and stifle unmercifully their greatest gift to our children—their ability to be creative.

*     *     *

I've heard the fear voiced several times and from various sources that an excellent teacher will become an administrator and thus will be lost to the children. This doesn't happen too often because not all teachers want to be administrators.   This is difficult for some supervisors to understand, believing as they do that being elevated to their level is the be-all/end-all for a teacher.  It is not.

The be-all/end-all occurs in our classrooms when our students' eyes light up with pleasure as they catch the meaning of some concept for the first time or when they feel good about themselves because they've just succeeded at something.  Our reward comes in our classroom as we watch our children laugh and learn. And in that order.

## l)  <u>**Evaluate teacher training and make changes.**</u>

Many articles on educational reform focus on the factual knowledge of teachers, which is important.  Equally important, however, is knowing how to transfer this knowledge to their students; how to make learning fun, interesting, and challenging; and how to instill in them an eagerness to return to class the following day.  I've had to defend this several times because there are those who say knowledge is everything.

In a high school algebra class my teacher asked for questions and I pointed out a problem that stretched almost across the whole page of my book.  He copied it across the whole blackboard, stepped back, and said, "Oh, I see what that is."  He wrote some short answer under the problem, and with no further instruction, dismissed the class.  He was a most knowledgeable person in algebra.  He did not know how to teach.

If I suddenly had to teach a sixth-grade class on world geography, I might have to review a few things before beginning.  Just as important to me, however, would be that my children leave my classroom eager to return the following day to see what I was going to do that would be equally as interesting.

College training for teachers should include semester-long courses on pedagogy.  Teacher curricula should also include instruction on the value and necessity of rapport, laughter, conscientiousness and empathy.  When a child loves the teacher and the teacher loves the child, we have the most fertile ground for learning.  A good rapport between teacher and child is readily detectable.  In addition to the value this brings to children, the existence of a good rapport is the easiest way for a principal to determine how well teachers are communicating with their children.  This is one thing that cannot be faked or called into being only when the teacher is being observed.

Along with rapport, conscientiousness and empathy are the mother and father of all good teaching.  Conscientious teachers will do what is best for the children, whether or not they are being watched by evaluators. Empathetic teachers understand what their children are feeling. This keeps them in tune with what each child needs and prevents them from feeling superior or inciting fear.

Perhaps the most crucial element of good teaching is to arouse in children a desire to learn. This is the catalyst that will serve to inspire them to "reach" for knowledge, which will make their lives richer for as long as they live.

As for laughter, strong evidence supports the benefits of laughter to life, health, and healing. Equally well known is that everyone learns better under conditions of pleasure. Should it be a surprise, then, that laughter produces its greatest benefits in the classroom? Shakespeare would agree and probably call it yesterday's news. He wrote it centuries ago in Tranio's words in <u>The Taming of the Shrew</u>, "No profit grows where is no pleasure taken."


## 2) <u>Allow the lead teacher in a grade level to attend teachers' interviews.</u>

If a first-grade teacher is being interviewed for a first-grade position, the lead teacher for the first-grade should be present. The information presented in Chapter Two indicates that administrators are not always completely qualified to set the educational policy; yet they are the ones hiring teachers.

I recognize, however, that it is difficult (even for a discerning interviewer) to determine whether a person will be a good teacher. Some teachers talk a good game, but just because they are adult-friendly doesn't mean they will care about children. The lead teacher in the grade level for which the applicant is being considered will be of great help to the (nonteacher) administrator during the interview. Significant questions must be asked, and if teachers wishing to be hired don't understand about children needing to work from success or if they are not familiar with the principles of readiness, then they are not ready to teach.

3) **<u>Allow good teachers to be their own creative selves</u>**.

Teachers who have devised good seatwork that has proven to be effective should not be forced to follow a plan devised for incompetent teachers.  Nor should they be forced to follow a supervisor's "new" plan unless it is educationally sound.


4) **<u>Principals must observe, document and fire incompetent teachers.</u>**

Principals must observe their teachers and document what they see.  If a teacher is incompetent, the visits must be repeated and the data recorded.  The principal might also have the superintendent observe also.  At this point, the incompetent teacher must be dismissed.  Since it falls to the principals to dismiss teachers, they should also be included in the hiring process.


5) **<u>Redesign the hierarchial organization of a school system.</u>**

The system of evaluation regarding the placement of children must be redesigned wherever participants (nurses, psychologists, supervisors, superintendents, personnel directors, educational consultants, supervisors of supervisors, etc.) believe they are isolated unto themselves within their field of expertise. No, teachers are not trained in those fields.  What we ask is that a communal, collaborative, contributory spirit prevail in any conference called to decide upon the disposition of a child, and the teacher should be considered a key, integral member of this team.


**<u>One last thought.</u>**

The children are the most important members of the school process and system. Teachers are the next most important.  That the current educational system does not recognize this is apparent in the priorities set by a school district. We know what these priorities are by the conditions in which many of our children sit and by the conditions under which many of our teachers work versus the affluent conditions within which many administrators operate.

In some school districts, regardless of their financial situations, the budget includes a six percent raise for the superintendent every year plus whatever percentage raise teachers receive. In a year when teachers receive a two percent raise, the superintendent receives an eight percent increase. In a year when teachers receive no increase, the superintendent receives six percent. The question is this: Isn't this backwards? Which brings us to money.

# Chapter 6

The Money:  Benefits and Perks—But Not for the Children


> "The way to stop financial joy-riding is to arrest
> the chauffeur and not the automobile."
> — Woodrow Wilson


In a statement made to the country during his Educational Summit, former President Bush called to our attention a key word—accountability.  Whereas the first step in this book involves looking at some of the problems (which may have included some rather uncomfortable reading), the second step involves looking at accountability and how it concerns each of us.  You may be among those doing the planning or the spending or among those doing the taking or the paying. In either case, you will find yourselves in this chapter—at a crossroads and called upon to make a decision. Should we continue at our present rate of academic decline; or should we actively work for change, dealing with all problem areas openly, honestly, and without regard for self?

While reading this chapter, the thought to hold is this: The money designated for education belongs to the children—all of it. We adults have been entrusted, on our honor, to spend the children's money wisely and well on their behalf. As you read, picture what could be done in classrooms with the billions of dollars we shall find wasted on unnecessary positions, offices, labs, and salaries from Federal offices, to State Departments of Education, to local school districts. For the children's sake, then, it is time to eliminate the waste; however, we must first determine where and why it occurs.


## It's the Waste That Angers

Parents and taxpayers find themselves in a distressing situation. They want to support their educational system, but the waste angers them. They struggle with ever-increasing tax burdens in districts with ever-decreasing test scores. Taxpayers are seeing that for all their sacrificial paying they are reaping negative results. Results that affect other areas of their lives.

For example, some businesses have difficulty filling positions because of a lack of skills on the part of their applicants. When young persons seeking jobs are not properly educated, the training falls upon corporations. This training costs millions of dollars a year. The question to taxpayers, then, is this: Do these corporations bear the full brunt of all those dollars spent in education or is this expense passed on to us, the consumers? And if so, then aren't taxpayers paying for the same education twice? They paid for the education the children did not get in school, and now they're paying for their education in the business world.

One angry parent told me, "Some of our administrators make over $250 a day, and now they're charging me a lot of student and extracurricular fees."

Then taxpayers read reports like this:

> "Property taxes up 89 percent in decade .... The primary reason is voters' approval of new tax levies and bond issues ..."[1]

In the same city, this same newspaper reported:

> "Sick days become retirement bonanza."

One Public School Superintendent was retiring:

> " ... with an extra $100,000 in his pocket, money accumulated over the years as compensation for unused sick time. If he worked for most other Ohio school districts, his compensation for the same amount of unused sick days would be $16,850."[2]

In all states, in many school districts, we find situations of incredible waste. For example, in one district, over 140 administrators were found to be unnecessary. One administrator, who had kept his position for over 25 years, admitted the system had gotten top heavy. When we multiply all these salaries by years of service and by 140 and then add all the unnecessary salaries that still exist in this district, we find an incredible amount of wasted money. This list must include not just the salaries, but all the expense of supporting the bureaucracy, including office space, equipment, computers, secretaries, etc. How honorably, then, are we acting in situations like these, or how ethically?


## The Waste Also Angers Teachers

Some teachers may disagree, but I personally have never worked with a teacher who minded not receiving a raise if the school district was truly in financial difficulty and no excessive waste existed. Nor have I worked with teachers in poorer districts who resented buying school supplies out of their own pockets when everyone else was also making sacrifices.

Teachers from one school, however, explained to me what they do mind. Believing that everyone was making sacrifices they said they had agreed not to take a raise for the next school year. Midyear they learned that administrators were not only given raises, but that the raises were made retroactive. This they minded.

In another district there were so many unnecessary administrators that teachers felt the only hope to change the situation was to make the parents aware of where the waste occurs because, although teachers are helpless, the parents could protest. Their quandary was how to make the parents aware of this inside information. Finally they decided to make the duplication in function and unnecessary expense known by posting an administrators' salary schedule in a lunchroom that teachers shared with volunteer parents. Within 20 minutes it had been removed. They posted another, and then another. Within one week, several posted salary schedules had mysteriously disappeared.

In another district, the superintendent eliminated many teaching positions, which drastically increased the size of classes. At a board meeting, the teachers explained how detrimental this was to the learning process and asked why some administrative cuts could not be made instead. An administrator's answer shows the administrative mindset. She said that to cut administrators would be to defy all common sense and logic. Teachers want to know what it defies when young children are expected to learn in larger and larger classes. Whatever that logic is, an explanation is long overdue—to the taxpayers, to the teachers, and to the children.


## <u>Shouldn't We Trustees Look at the Salaries?</u>

As trustees of the children's money, it is time for us to focus on salaries and perks. Although there are others that are even more excessive, one such salary gives us the picture. This action took place midyear when board members voted to raise their superintendent's salary. That salary included:

> "... a raise of 5 percent to $129,591, retroactive to August 1. He also gets a $5,000 car allowance, $6,400 expense account, $400,000 in life insurance, and 27 days of vacation. The district pays $7,988 of his $11,922 annual retirement contribution, and will pay it all after August 1."[3]

In my years of interviewing and collecting information, until recently I rarely saw an administrators' salary schedule posted anywhere. There's probably a very good reason for that. What would the public do if they saw the number of salaries per district, not to mention the size of some of those salaries.

While visiting in one city, a group of teachers told me about an administrator who was upset because her salary of $99,500 had been published inaccurately. She said that her salary had been reported at $106,000 and that figure had made citizens angry. She wanted the correct figure to be published and the error to be explained to the public.

One teacher explained, "This is not a huge, profit-making corporation paying these salaries—ours is a struggling school district." So her salary isn't $106,000. So her salary is $99,500. Okay, we'll buy that. Forget about explaining the $106,000. Explain the $99,500.

Reprinted with special permission of King Features Syndicate     4

## <u>For Friends Also</u>

Another prevalent practice takes place when the public or a research committee "catches on" to the duplication in function among administrators.  When they receive complaints, some superintendents will let these administrators go (with large incentives to leave).  Their positions will be eliminated from the books.  Then they will be hired back as  contract employees with salaries being drawn from a different account.  The Superintendent then appears to have been responsive to the public's outcry.  So, are we now back to the way we were, paying for unnecessary positions?  Well, not quite.  We're now also out the cost of the incentives to leave.  It gets worse.

## Can Anyone Explain to Me the Decadent Buy-outs?

I can explain the "what"; it's the "why" I would like explained to me.  Buy-outs happen when School Boards give superintendents who are still an unknown quantity a multiyear contract, and after it is signed, find them to be wrong for the position.  Some local districts set their minimums at three years.  This means, then, that no matter how incompetent administrators turn out to be, they stay for three years unless the district buys out the contract.

Some school boards give in when a superintendent insists on a six-year contract.  Some of these result in million-dollar (or greater) buy-outs because the choice then becomes: Either teachers and children suffer under poor leadership for a number of years, or the district takes hundreds of thousands of dollars from the funds designated for education to make these superintendents wealthy for no services.

Sometimes the buy-out is a "flat-out" gift.  Sometimes the superintendent is required to "do" something. For example, some buy-outs are camouflaged by promises that  superintendents will visit the district during the year and give some advisory input from time to time to earn the money paid to them.  The assumption is that the public will not be wise enough to ask why these superintendents were fired if their input was worth hundreds of thousands of dollars.

In one school district, the "surplus" superintendent was required to report in each day while another superintendent was on the job.  The intent here is to give the public the impression that the district is obtaining the services of both superintendents, but the bottom line is simply this—some districts pay two superintendents for the services of one, sometimes for several years.

One superintendent left with a buy-out package of $172,000.  When the courts determined that this was illegal, some private citizens stepped forward and paid out the contract for her.  This unnecessary expense took place in a district where some classrooms were in an advanced state of disrepair.  Another superintendent, who had insisted on a six-year contract, had the contract bought out for a half-million dollars.  In another large city, the buy-out of one superintendent's contract cost its taxpayers one million dollars. The cost of some buy-outs are even greater.

In addition to the size of the buy-outs, some parents become angry because the deed is done before they are informed. Speaking of a buy-out in his district one parent said, "By the time I knew about it, the     superintendent was gone with the money—one million dollars to be exact."

Should we feel better about this practice of buy-outs when citizens step in and provide the funds? Not really. What could these same funds do to change some of the deplorable situations in which our children sit?

These buy-outs show the ability of some superintendents to "wheel and deal" successfully on their own behalf. Can anyone explain to me or to taxpayers such incredible remunerative rewards for the simple service of having been found unsuitable or incompetent? When we give away millions upon millions of education dollars to this practice, can we say we've acted wisely or ethically with the funds entrusted to our keeping and to our discretion?


## **Lost and Found**

Sometimes the money is just lost. Hard-pressed taxpayers then have to pay for a management audit to find out that the money has simply disappeared. The cost of the audit adds greatly to the cost of the loss, sometimes half as much again as the money that has disappeared.

Sometimes the money is found. In one district the superintendent promised cuts if the levy did not pass. It didn't. Then suddenly, almost two million dollars was found, and the cuts didn't have to be made. The superintendent knew about the "found" money before the levy vote but did not tell the voters. Needless to say, this caused a furor of some proportion.

Reprinted with special permission of King Features Syndicate5

## **But We've Spent All Our Money on Baubles; Now We Need Money For Food**

And now the needs are real—the children's needs, that is.  The educational system, however, is not always an equal opportunity company.  The administrators get the huge salaries, the benefits, the buy-outs, the perks, and the cushy jobs.  Depending on the school district, the children get school buildings with crumbling infrastructures, pulpy ceilings, windows that leak, and insufficient funds for their school supplies, at-risk programs, books, bus service, and (sometimes), even for enough heat to keep them warm.

Once again, we find ourselves facing the dilemma of adult wants taking precedence over the children's need.  While many of the administrators' wants were not necessary, they took a great deal of the money.  The children's needs are very real, but not enough money is left to meet them. Real or not, an over-taxed public is tired of hearing about it.


## A Different Vocabulary

Tired or not, taxpayers are called upon to add one more tax burden to their limited incomes. The guilt tactics begin, and the rhetoric changes. Suddenly, we begin to hear the word "children," which we did not hear during salary negotiations or during buy-out decisions for administrators. The poor children. Absolutely. Help the children. Certainly. Children sit in dangerous buildings and play on unsafe playground equipment. I'm afraid so.

As the campaign heats up, we read about those stingy people who do not care enough about children to pass levies. When all else fails, children are drawn into the fray. Their pleas are touching and sometimes heartbreaking. They sometimes carry signs or write letters to their newspapers. One child said he had given all his savings to keep his good teacher from being dismissed. Heartbreaking indeed.

Regardless of the rhetoric, the implied equation is this—vote for every tax levy or you are against children. For the most part, this is not the case. Most people who do not vote for school levies either simply cannot afford to raise their property taxes one more time, or they are cognizant of how the tax money they are sacrificing is being spent and they disapprove.

Sometimes outside influences prevail. A well-known politician came to stump for a school tax levy in my city, where he neither lives nor pays property tax. In fact, he didn't stay long enough to see if an increased tax rate was really the answer. Yet we were told he had made a difference. After the levy was passed, placing some taxpayers perilously close to having to sell their homes, the politician left to live outside our tax burdened area. Regarding the issue of the elderly on fixed incomes or those who have lost their jobs, the comment is merely, "Well, that is touching, but unfortunate."

<u>**Yet Another Fallacy**</u>

The general belief has been that the more money a school district has, the better the children's academic performance will be. This is not necessarily so.

> "A 1992 U.S. Department of Education press release observed the following: 'In spite of the increased investment in education spending by all levels of government in recent years, there has been no corresponding improvement in student achievement.
>
> "For example, in 1960 we spent $16 Billion per year on education and our schools were the envy of the world. In 1990 we spent $200 billion and our schools are among the worst of the industrialized nations.' "[6]

By this time, we've all seen studies that show no relationship between student cost and student scores. In some cases, the group doing the research was amazed. Teachers probably weren't.

Why is there no relationship between scores and money? The reasons are numerous. Money cannot make the sow's ear of mainstreaming into the silk purse of successful learning. Money cannot foster healthy self images in children. Money cannot substitute anything more worthy to fill the terrible void left by a lack of phonetic instruction. Money does not rid a district of incompetent teachers. Money is too often used for salaries and too seldom used to provide smaller classes. Money does not promote the concept of empathy for one's "neighbor." And finally, whereas a smaller, poorer school district does not have as much money for supplies, equipment, or salaries, neither does it have the money for numerous administrators who set the policy, the tone, and in some cases, the stress level for teachers. I have worked in both situations.

In one small town, I taught in a poor school district where the teachers actually bought all the supplies for the children. A parent who was moving to the area told me how upset and anxious she was. Her son would be transferring to our small rural school from a school district in one of our largest cities, which had a tremendous budget. She asked how I would address the disparity between the two school programs—would I be able to challenge him and still teach to my "country" students?

I assured her I would provide the necessary course work to keep him challenged, but I suggested that we first find what that "disparity" was. Her child proved to be behind my students in every subject area. Thus, rather than keeping him challenged because he was so far ahead, it became a matter of remediating him because he was so far behind.

The following year, in this same school district, a teacher turned book salesperson came to sell the district a new reading program that would "teach children many new words and concepts not normally found in a regular reading series." She demonstrated this advanced lesson in my classroom. My children knew all the words and the meanings which undermined her presentation. She was not pleased. She hinted at the possibility (well, it was a little more than a hint) that I had seen this new program beforehand and had prepared the children, although she couldn't see how. I assured her I had never seen the program.

The point is this. Never (before or since I held this position) was I allowed to be as fully creative as I am capable of being. Nor was I ever as free to take my children as far as I could—happily! I had no supervisor (except my principal), no restrictions, no fancy equipment, no computers, and no interference. And no money!


## Where We Stand

The situation is bleak. Even State governments that have historically balanced budgets are spending more than they collect in taxes. Education, welfare, and crime are among the largest drains on taxpayers. Our challenge is this: If we can fix the one (education), we could eliminate some of the other two (welfare and crime). Yes, I realize many other factors are involved here;

however, no one can deny the role that lack of education plays in all our social ills.

One prevalent philosophy states that we may have to hit rock bottom before we can effect a radical change so necessary in education. Therefore, we may have to stop passing levies that barely keep the system alive and thereby delay the needed reforms. I understand this and believe that we are rapidly approaching this state of affairs whether we believe in this philosophy or not. Why? Because taxpayers are quite simply "taxed out."

We have consistently tried to heal education's major illnesses with first-aid measures. It is easier to "patch" than to get to the real reasons for the problem, to perform major reconstructive surgery, and then to wait for the healing and its results. When we find that "quick-fix" tax levies are insufficient, we turn to the Federal Government for more and more money. We elect presidents based on their promises to further bankrupt our country for education, despite the fact that, to a large extent, we already have the needed money. It's just being mismanaged, which we can also change.

Does the situation seem hopeless? It isn't. The first thing to understand is that administrators are sitting in the catbird's seat. They make the decisions about their incomes and benefits, and convince the school boards that these decisions are necessary and proper. But at levy time, they cry, "Children, children! Remember the children!" Un-uh.
Because apple pie, motherhood, and schools have been somewhat regarded as the "sacred cows" of our society, those in power in the educational system stand behind this protective shield of "schools," and they have been at liberty to devise and institute all kinds of benefits for themselves. Let us keep the apple pie, and motherhood; however, every administrator (state, Federal, and local) must step forward and be scrutinized, and judged by those who are paying (the taxpayers) for the sake of those who are losing (the children).

There are ways to assess your school district. If administrators are honest, open and aboveboard in the operation of their school districts, allowing citizens to look at the financial sheets and the administrative services presents no problem. On the other hand, if they have something to hide, they are likely to resist the investigative procedure. Perhaps this equates to: The harder they resist, the more they have to hide.

*     *     *

Put them all together, and they spell culpability. One of the purposes of this book is to group information together in one place so you can see the full extent of the problem. The following grouping presents only a few of the financial advantages Federal, State, and local administrators envision, devise, incorporate, and grant themselves.

- Exorbitant salaries.

- Incredible perks that can include car phones or country club memberships.

- Multiyear contracts.

- Preventing reassignment to a lower salaried position.

- Sick leave paid on retirement that is many times over State limits.

- Expense accounts.

- Hundreds of thousands of unnecessary positions — Federal, State and local.

- Buy-outs.

- Huge paid-up life insurance policies.

- Car Allowances.

Can anyone look at this partial list of what many of those in charge have provided for themselves, what many school boards under duress have agreed to grant them, and what we citizens have allowed school boards to grant, and say that we have acted responsibly or wisely with our children's money?  How about honorably?

## 1) <u>Act!</u>

In response to my inquiry, one principal said, "Oh, but everyone knows about the administrator problem. That's not going to change because there's nothing we can do about it." Public unawareness is no doubt one of the reasons we have not as yet acted as a nation to change this situation. Although citizens are aware that waste occurs, they are not aware of the full extent of this abuse of the children's monies. Another reason we have not acted may be that school boards have been threatened with the fact that costly superintendents are the only ones who have enough charisma to convince voters to pass levies. Do not fall for this.

Here another vicious circle emerges. If we didn't have such high-priced administrators we wouldn't need to pass so many levies. I personally have known some excellent principals who became superintendents and for little more than their principal's salary. They knew the district, the teachers, and the children. In addition to their lack of greed and their common-sense approach, this knowledge helped them do a masterful job. While not every principal could serve in this capacity, this is a source of talent worth the consideration of school boards in their search for superintendents.

## 2) <u>Don't fall for the numbers either.</u>

Don't let school officials convince you they need a huge staff, when they do not. A large district in one state had a superintendent who ran the district beautifully for years with a treasurer and some secretaries. He had time to walk about the school buildings and visit with teachers and students. When he retired a new superintendent arrived on the scene at a much larger salary. One by one he began to add to the administrative staff, although enrollment had begun to drop. In time, this superintendent had three assistant superintendents, a personnel director, twelve supervisors, a supervisor of supervisors, two educational consultants, and a budget that required the annual passing of levies. All this and fewer students.


## 3) <u>**Demand accountability.**</u>

Sometimes we find that political manuverings can keep accountability confused and uncertain—even nonexistent—when the superintendent is a fast talker.  The members of the  citizen's group mentioned in Chapter 3 are the ones who must look into the finances of the school districts.  I warn you of two things here: 1) you may be unhappily surprised, and 2) your administrators may resist this procedure.

Parents complain about a lack of openness on the part of the school board and superintendents. Some superintendents often give the impression that they can keep this information private and diligently try to do so; however, the passage of the Sunshine Law, allows citizens to look.  Therefore, citizens' groups can break through.  One parent who tried to look into the financial situation in her district said of her experience, "It was like trying to break through a brick wall." True.  Nevertheless, brick walls can be taken apart—one brick at a time if necessary.


## 4) <u>**Study successful districts.**</u>

Some districts go years without an operating levy.  Find them, and see how they manage this.  For example, one thing such a district will do is spend a one-time grant on a one-time project. When districts spend one-time grants on staff, the staff member still has to be paid after the money is gone.  The successful districts will be happy to share the reasons for their success.

5) **<u>Make the system work for us rather than against us.</u>**

When a citizens' group is diligently working to reform their school system, the State department may (or may not) back off from some of the bureaucratic requirements that tend to hinder the reform process. When one citizens' group did an intensive study of their school system, they discovered a bloated, centralized administration and wasted dollars. Because it was a large metropolitan school district, this discovery received a great deal of publicity. As a result, the State made concessions and the system was pared down so that it became more effective and efficient.

Citizens' groups must investigate their school systems because they can do successfully what State Departments of Education (so far removed from the local districts) are unable to do. This action can cause the State to back off, and the resulting reduction in school-related bureaucracies will free up more money for its intended use—better education.

In other words, like the ripples that go out from a pebble thrown into the water, waste could be eliminated by the ripples that begin at the local levels, move to the State levels, and continue on to Federal levels. The citizens' groups are the pebbles.

The district just discussed was large. Lacking the same political influence or clout, smaller districts might not get the same media coverage. Should these smaller school systems meet with resistance, it might become necessary somehow to involve the media.

6) **<u>Save money in every way possible.</u>**

In addition to eliminating all unnecessary administrators and supervisors, we might also eliminate not all, but some assistant principal positions. A principal's job is the most hectic at the beginning of the school year; however, when this levels off, many assistant principals do not have as much to do.

During a principal's busier times, substitute teachers, retired principals, retired teachers, part-time or "come-in-as-needed" secretaries could do this work. These workers would cost only a fraction of what it costs to maintain an unnecessary assistant principal.

Schools that have assistant principals with time on their hands might consider using them to assist the teachers. For example, they could sit in classes when teachers are in conferences. One assistant principal scheduled a parent/psychologist/teacher conference for me during my normal classtime. I asked him if he would sit in my room while I was in the conference. I explained that the children would already have their work. His response was, "That's not my job." I reiterated that there would be nothing for him to do but sit there. When he shook his head, I asked him what I should do with my children while I was in the conference. His response, "That's not my job."

The teacher across the hall had to watch my class along with her own. No teaching took place in either classroom for that lenghty period of time.


## 7) <u>Eliminate multiyear contracts.</u>

No more multiyear contracts, at least until the superintendent is tried and proven.


## 8) <u>No more buy-outs.</u>

No more gifts that can reach a million dollars (or even greater) to make administrators a privileged group at the expense of the children. Taxpayers cannot afford to pay these huge rewards to employees for leaving a position. The system must stop providing multiyear contracts that can encumber school funds with such extraordinary outlays.


## 9) <u>Consider our most valuable assets.</u>

We might take note of one of Japan's philosophies, that their employees are their most valuable asset. Whenever we have tried to change our children's learning success based solely on directives from administrators; whenever we have tried to successfully run businesses based solely on directives from CEO's, presidents, and managers; and whenever we have tried to reform school systems based solely on directives from the President, governors, and State education officials, we have failed.

If we are honest and open with ourselves, we should now admit that the future success of our country is in doubt whenever we ignore the teachers, the workers, and the taxpayers. The country cannot operate successfully solely from the top down. Nor can it be financially sound.

# Chapter 7

Attitude:  The Heart of the Problem


"Fanatics are basically people who believe in a single cause of conditions and that if the cause was eliminated, the conditions would be rectified; whereas in reality all conditions are caused by a combination of influences, none of which alone will remedy the ailment."[1]

— Sydney J. Harris


Historian Jacob Burckhardt said, "Beware the terrible simplifier."  This is particularly apt with regard to educational reform.  The reasons for our educational dilemmas are numerous.

The problem is this: Whereas some of these reasons are obvious—the system itself, careerist administrators, irresponsible parents, incompetency, and money—others, such as attitude, are much more subtle. Both kinds of reasons, then, combine to form an alliance of influences that keep us enough at cross purposes that correct school reform procedures remain fragmented and obscure.

Attitudes that affect children adversely are difficult to uncover, more difficult to understand, and most difficult to change. Changing our attitudes usually requires attacking lifelong beliefs that can affect lifestyles or incomes, foregoing pride and greed wherever they affect learning, and scrutinizing (with total honesty) our innermost motives. NOW, we're talking "difficult."

This chapter explains how that self-interest-first attitudes are the single most fixed deterrent to educational reform. Reform in the schools is an impossible task until these attitudes change. Studying these attitudes brings us to the heart of the problem and, therefore, to the heart of the book.


## Everyone Is Affected

The first change in attitude involves those who believe that only parents of school-age children are affected by our nation's educational dilemmas. Such people say, "I'd like to help, but I'm not involved; my children are no longer in school."

Life in the 1990's is hectic and harried. So many things require our attention (not to mention our money) that we begin to categorize segments of society and fail to see how much one affects the other. This attitude says, "Education's over there, and goodness knows they have their troubles; but I'm over here, surrounded by my own pressing concerns." During a group discussion regarding our children's situation, one lady concluded, "Well, that's not my problem." But it is. Our educational failures affect everyone.

## <u>Illiteracy Reaches Out</u>

The failure of our educational system is the shot heard 'round the nation.  Education, or the lack thereof, affects every one of us in one capacity or another, whether as parent, child, worker, taxpayer, consumer, voter, citizen, politician, teacher or victim.  For example, poor self-images can be the root cause of many crimes.  Sometimes persons become involved in crime partially because throughout their formative school years they were made to feel that they were failures.  In a crime situation, they feel powerful or in charge, perhaps for the first time in their lives.  Over half our country's prisoners are school dropouts.

Depending upon the state, it costs taxpayers far more to keep prisoners in jail than to keep a child in school.  Isn't it time to change the underlying attitude and make the connection—our social ills are affected by the quality of education.

To ignore this is to work from the same perspective as the woodcutter who worked harder all day than his partner and yet had cut far less wood.  He explained to his employer, "Well, my axe was dull, but I didn't want to take time out from my wood-cutting to sharpen it."

Illiteracy is the mother of welfare and the father of unemployment.  Therefore the question before us is this:  To what extent can we improve our social ills until we "take time out" to fix our educational system?  This is a crucial question.  Its answer will ultimately determine the course and fate of our nation.  It has always been this way.

> "All who have mediated on the art of governing mankind have been convinced that the fate of empires depends on the education of our youth."
>
> — Aristotle

> "Education is our only political safety.  Outside of this ark, all is deluge."
>
> — Horace Mann

Are Americans not finding this to be true?  We are flooded with rising crime rates to the point where we lead all industrialized nations in violent crimes.  We are flooded with flagrant drug use, exorbitant taxes, concerns regarding welfare and unemployment numbers, and more and more children who are depressed, violent, illiterate, and uneducated.

Some children plan their own funerals.  They suspect they will not grow up because they have seen so many of their friends die from gunfire.  Some schools have installed metal detectors, surveillance cameras, and motion detectors.  If we read an article, a book, a research study, a newspaper, or magazine (sometimes even a comic strip), we cannot miss the connection between poor educational skills and our other social ills.  Nor can we miss the connection between increasing youth crime and decreasing test scores.


## The Children

The most important and difficult change in underlying attitudes concerns the children.  This very necessary change is difficult because it is neither tangible nor visible; and is, above all else, subtle.  We say the right words, but the attitudes have brought us to our present condition.

Listening to the words "We love our children" (and assuming that all adults do) has allowed attitudes to work silently and wreak havoc upon children without being readily detected.  The underlying attitudes, however, leave a trail.  What we finally see and are eventually left with, is the aftermath.

Let us evaluate the situation.  First, consider how safe our children are or how well cared for.  How well are they educated? How emotionally stable or psychologically sound are they?  How many are abused, suicidal, guilt-ridden, menacing, and depressed? What about manners? How kind are they to their peers and teachers? What about their social and moral values?  The answers to these questions form the trail, and all of them affect learning.

In today's society, many children are treated as unimportant second-class citizens.  Too often there is little regard for their feelings and even less for their rights.  There is also a general all-around failure to understand what children need to flourish.  Far too many adults believe that children are just these little unintuitive people running around, who can't feel, fear, process, understand, or relate to adults until they are somewhere around sixteen or so.


## The Words—the Attitude—the Aftermath

Despite the words we say underlying attitudes affect children and learning in today's classrooms.  Bob Keeshan, who played Captain Kangaroo on television for decades, had this to say at a rally in Missouri.

> "Handle kids with care… children are the nation's infrastructure and half of them are at risk of leaving school, being abused and suffering physical or emotional problems.

> "The rhetoric of America—'We love our children'—is not the reality of America.  'Wake up, politicians!  Become statesmanlike!  Tomorrow is too late.'"[2]

He's right.  In far too many cases, love (although professed) is not the reality.  The following are some examples of this.

The words are, "We love our children."  Nevertheless, the underlying attitudes result in millions of children not being fed properly or clothed warmly.  In the aftermath, we find these children ill much of the school year, suffering from horrible coughs and runny noses.  Miserable and lethargic, such children do not learn well.

The words are, "The welfare of my child is all important." Wonderful words, but what the underlying attitude produces is many children being emotionally, physically, and sexually abused. In the aftermath, we see these children living in dread and fear, going to bed with several layers of clothing on to protect them against what is going to happen to them again, and then again. When they are awake they are exhausted; when they are asleep they have nightmares. How well do you believe any of these children learn?

The words are, "Certainly my child has rights." The underlying attitude, however, produces expectant parents who smoke, drink, and take drugs, even though they know the horrifying effects these actions can have on the fetus and then on the newborn. Although it is completely preventable, Fetal Alcohol Syndrome is the leading known cause of retardation. Where are these children's rights? What kind of learners will they be?

Also, if children grow up in homes with alcoholic parents, they may become codependent. This produces low self-esteem in children, which also affects learning.

The words are, "Our children's safety is our primary concern." Yet many times the underlying attitude produces the difficult-to-understand premise that those who commit atrocities against children should receive light sentences (if any) and be freed to commit those atrocities again and yet again.

Intent also plays a part in this unfathomable reasoning. If the attacker didn't intend to pick up the baseball bat and kill the child, well, okay then—just so it wasn't premeditated. In the aftermath, children live in horrifying circumstances where brutal beatings can blind, deafen, or cripple them (emotionally and physically). If they are not mortally wounded and manage to survive to sit in classrooms, they do not learn well.

In my classrooms I have watched such children; they tended to be nervous, distrustful, sad, sluggish, listless, frightened, tired or too quiet. Some cried easily; some were stoic. Some fell asleep in class, had dark circles under their eyes, and were not prepared to concentrate. It was impossible for some of them to learn, certainly not to their full potential.

"We want our children to do well in school." Those are the words, but the attitude sends some parents into schools dictating directives regarding discipline and learning. This attitude produces children who are belligerent, frustrated, unruly, irresponsible, embarrassed or emotionally stressed. All of these things greatly affect learning.


## The Underlying Attitudes Carry Over

It is a very short step, then, from the prevailing attitude that adults are more important than children in the homes and in the courts to the position that they are also more important in the schools. Therefore, even though the whole educational venture is inordinately unsuccessful, many leaders still believe they deserve to have their prestige up front and their money off the top. Because they are adults.

Administrators say, "Our schools are designed to promote learning and self-worth. We put our children first." Yet attitude clearly enters into how the lines in a school district are drawn. For example, in a district where I taught, as enrollment began falling, the dirty, dingy, hot classrooms (emptied of children) were beautifully renovated with wood-paneling, carpeting, and air-conditioning and then became offices for administrators. As I stepped into one of the renovated rooms, I remembered how, in that very room, my students had sweltered in some months and shivered in others.

Cartoonist Marshall Clark illustrated the disrepair that we find in many of today's schools.

Reprinted with permission by Marshall Clark    3

What this picture illustrates comes perilously close to becoming a reality in many school districts.

Observing this transformation from poverty for the children to luxury for the administrators, I was reminded of the poem, "The Plaint of the Camel" by Charles Edward Carryl.  It reads in part:

> "Canary Birds feed on sugar and seed,
>     Parrots have crackers to crunch;
> And, as for the poodles, they tell me
>     the noodles,
> Have chicken and cream for their lunch.
>         But there's never a question,
>         About MY digestion—

ANYTHING does for me!
"Cats, you're aware, can repose in a chair,
Chickens can roost upon rails,
Puppies are able to sleep in a stable,
and oysters can slumber in pails.
But no one supposes
A poor camel dozes—
ANY PLACE does for me!

"Lambs are enclosed where it's never exposed,
Coops are constructed for hens;
Kittens are treated to houses well heated,
And pigs are protected by pens.
But a Camel comes handy
Wherever its sandy—
ANYWHERE does for me!"

Children and teachers understand the plaint of the camel.


## Some Parents Understand Also

Reflective of the this attitude, we see how worried parents with struggling children are treated by some administrators. The following two interviews with parents are presented verbatim.

### Interview Number 1

"I wanted to believe what these school people said. I had two other children who went through the system with no problems whatever. I thought it was a wonderful system. I now know that you cannot know a system until you have a problem.

"My third child had a slight speech problem. His kindergarten teacher told me at the end of the year that he was not reading. Therefore he was probably learning-disabled. I said I didn't know children had to be reading in kindergarten.  She told me my son knew his ABC's but was a total nonreader.  Because of that, he was going to be put in a 'whole language' classroom for the first grade. I asked what that meant.  She said, 'No phonics.'

"This doubled his trouble.  With his speech problem he would say 'tool bus.'  Therefore, in first grade, he would spell it 'tool bus.'  Soon he began to hate school.  By the first of January he was so frustrated that I decided to ask that he be tested.  I was told, 'We'll see.'

"By the end of January, no word had come from the school.  I contacted them again and insisted that my child be tested.  They said they 'would see.'  By the middle of February, when still nothing had been done, I requested intervention.  This is a process, in our district, where the principal, assistant principal, psychologist, and teachers talk, interview, test, and come together to decide what is best for the child.  The report is then given in a conference with the parents.

"In requesting intervention, I had mentioned that the first-grade teacher had been sending home tapes of her reading sessions with my son, but I explained that the classroom noise was so loud that I couldn't hear what they were saying.

"The report said: 1. The noise in the room did not bother my son.  He seems oblivious to it, he is so involved in his work.  2. He is small in stature.  3. He has poor social skills.

"The last point tipped me off.  This child is the most gregarious of children.  He's the one who brings home all his friends, even those in the grades above him.  He plays on a knothole ball team. He is constantly with friends.  I began to ask questions.

"I asked the psychologist, 'How much time did you spend with my son to come up with this information in your report?'

"He looked around the room at the others, then said, 'I've never met your boy.' Then I asked, 'Well, how much time did you spend observing him?' He had never observed him. His student psychologist had done the observing.

"I turned to the student psychologist and asked her how much time she had spent observing. She said she had watched from the doorway for about 15 minutes. But she had not spoken to him.

"I could see the principal, assistant principal, and psychologist wanted to divert the way this was going. They agreed that I was not spending enough time with my son at night. I told them how many hours each night we spent on his lessons. They then said that probably I was spending too much time with him each night.

"They said they would have a meeting and decide what could be done to help the child. At this point in the meeting, I found out the date on which they said my child had been observed. We had been out of town, and he was not even in school that day.

"With that, I lost it—blew my top. I told them that as far as helping children, they were a joke. My husband kept trying to quiet me down. The problem was that he had not lived through all the excuses I'd been given for six months now. He had no idea what all I'd gone through. We had a terrible fight that night. And in the end, he apologized. But all further communication from the school was addressed to him.

"Following the meeting, the remedial reading teacher told me it would do no good to get a private tutor. My son was too far behind, and I would just go broke to no avail.

"I considered suing them all, but a Board Member called me and told me to back down. 'If you don't,' she said, 'they'll just take it out on your children.' She said, 'I backed down once with my children—that's why I ran for this Board. But if a parent makes this system look bad, they don't like it, and they make you sorry.'

"This proved to be true. The next year, they put my son in another 'whole language' room, even though I had requested that he be in a room where phonics were taught.

"They finally came up with a solution for my son. They decided that if it took the other children 15 minutes to do a project, and my son 20 minutes to do it, he would have the extra time deducted from his recess. Keep in mind that my son could not read. It was going to take him a lot longer than five minutes to do the work of those who could read. And the reading teacher suggested we hold him back a year.

"I enrolled him in a reading recovery program at $100 a week. When he first entered, he was at a Level 7-9. First grade would be Level 16. The teacher was skeptical that she could bring him along far enough to go on to second grade.

"Six weeks later, he was at Level 28. He is working fine now in third grade, where they have just admitted—finally—that he has a speech problem. He will be going to speech therapy.

"Oh, one more thing. As I was talking to my son's new teacher for the second grade, the psychologist walked by. Looking at me, he said under his breath to the teacher, 'Good luck!'"

Whereas this parent just happened to catch on when the phrase "poor social skills" was used, there were other things for any trained professional to see. Not the least of these was the fact that any child who could work through such noise and be able to concentrate and try to do his work in spite of the fact that he couldn't read was a mature child capable of learning. Many parents are not given such good clues to refute the "experts," nor do many parents have the money to remediate their children. So where does this leave all the children caught in this situation, which is not an isolated case? Not only have I watched such situations, I've been a part of them.

<u>Interview Number 2</u>

I met this particular mother at a craft booth in a mall. She was crying and explaining to a friend what was happening to her little boy. When she turned away, I introduced myself and asked if I could use her story in my book. Again, this is verbatim.

"My little boy was the best child I'd ever seen until he began having trouble in school. And then, suddenly he was becoming a discipline problem.

"I spoke to his teacher, who finally, after months of my pushing, said we'd have him tested. They did, and he missed being in a L.D. (Learning Disabled) Class by one point. I asked them, 'Couldn't a test be off by that much?' But they said they wouldn't give on the score.

"Things worsened and finally I asked if, since he could not attend L.D. classes, couldn't we hold him back a year so he could catch up. They said no, his grades weren't F's, they were D's. They couldn't retain a child that was not failing.

"I'm so upset. I can't stop crying. My child is caught in between. One point on the L.D. test, and one grade on being retained. Now he's a real discipline problem, my good little boy."

The whole focus of a school system is supposed to be the children. Those are the words. They are seldom the reality.


## **<u>Avoidance</u>**

Avoidance is another underlying attitude that allows us to live more comfortably with direr issues. Avoidance is sometimes used even by those who are trying to help. Those reporters trying to jolt the public write of cuts for the schools; or of experts who draw grim a picture for today's schools; or of schools' tragic situations;

151

or of how school scores worsen.

Is it easier to face our problems if we think about these things happening to a cold, impersonal school building? How much could we tolerate if we rewrote these phrases correctly? Shouldn't that be cuts for children; or experts draw grim picture for today's children; or the children's situation is tragic; or children's scores worsen?

Avoidance allows us to take many liberties with the truth. We have avoided looking at our children realistically. We have avoided looking at their limitations and possibilities realistically. Therefore, we have not provided for them realistically.

It is such a short step from the underlying attitudes we hold, to the positions we take, to the resulting actualizations within our children. It's an even shorter step from avoidance to lying to ourselves. Sydney J. Harris once said:

> "The lies we tell other people customarily don't hurt
> them as much as the lies we tell ourselves hurt us;
> lying to others is debasing, but lying to oneself is
> ultimately fatal."[3]

In the same way, the lies we tell ourselves concerning our children's well-being and education can be ultimately fatal to our children, to ourselves, and in the long run, to our country.

*     *     *

H. G. Wells said:

> "Civilization is a race between education and
> catastrophe."

Surely no one has failed to notice that education is losing. And attitude is the root cause.

### 1) <u>**Put ourselves in our children's places.**</u>

Before we adults make any move affecting children, let us put ourselves in their place. Let us feel their helplessness before adults—all kinds of adults. Let us feel their dread, their fear, their stress, and their frustration as they face all the injustices enacted against them. Let us visualize their lack of choices. Let us feel their pain.

### 2) <u>**Honestly scrutinize our attitudes regarding children.**</u>

All adults who come into contact with a child must scrutinize their attitudes to consider how much of what they do is for the good of the children and how much is for their own sakes. Without this honest appraisal of themselves and their motives, nothing will change.

### 3) <u>**Understand how our actions affect children.**</u>

We also need to acknowledge, with honesty, how injustices against our young and all adult actions toward children contribute to the type of learner, adult, parent, or human being they will become. The choices that adults make (regarding time, priorities, substance abuse, discipline, ethical behavior, divorce, etc.) affect children in all areas of their existence have a great impact on their lives and learning. And attitude is the catalyst.

Have our actions toward children been good? Have they been fair? Have they had the welfare of the children at heart? Have they been ethical—honorable? Have the children's needs come before adult wants? These are the hard questions that need to be answered. And nothing will change for our children until they are.

4) **<u>Avoid Avoidance</u>**

Say it like it is.  Our children are either not learning or not learning to their full potential.  Our unworkable system is failing.  Our country is hurting.  Now that we've had the courage to admit it, we can fix it—but only by working together—for our children's sakes.

# Chapter 8

Another Obstacle to Learning—But You Won't Like It

"When you educate a man in mind and not in morals, you educate a menace to society.  You can put a public school and university in the middle of every block of every city in America , but you'll never keep America from rotting morally by mere intellectual education.

"Education cannot be properly called education which neglects the most important parts of man's nature.  Partial education is far worse than none at all, if we educate the mind and not the soul."
— Theodore Roosevelt

These words are true.  It is also true that the United States now leads industrialized nations in murders, sexual assaults and other attacks of violence.  Indeed, violence causes so many deaths and injuries each year that it is now considered by some to be a public health epidemic.

It is time for all Americans to reason together and find some common ground where we can meet and agree on what to teach our children for their sakes, which can never be separated from our sakes or our country's future.  Am I going to push Bible reading and prayer in school?  No. Let's begin another way—a way that compromises no one's beliefs.


## A Tired Excuse That No Longer Plays

We hear, "It's the parents' job to teach morals, ethics, values and how to treat one's neighbor; and if they're so concerned about such things, let them take their children to the local church." Sounds good; however, since so many parents don't do what they should, we can no longer pretend this is our answer.

Far too many homes have no religious or moral standards, and the children from these homes grow up with the same attitudes as their parents.  In homes where life is meaningless and cheap, many children learn to accept this and everyone becomes a victim.  When parents take no responsibility for their actions, many children likewise take no responsibility for their actions.  If no ethical or moral training is received at home, many children fail to become ethical or moral adults.  If they are not taught to understand the value of life, many children believe it's okay to avenge themselves if someone angers them, or even to be the aggressors.  Where no respect is shown for others or self in the home, neither do children respect themselves, their teachers or their peers.  This attitude affects learning.

We have also tended to blame only the "bad" parents for this failure to teach morality and virtue.  Actually, far too many "good" parents (those who feed, clothe, care for their children physically and help them with homework) not only neglect to give any moral training, but fail to live moral lives before their children.  This is the "do as I say not as I do" method of child rearing.  This doesn't work either.

Surely the need for some teaching of the principles that consider another's worth is apparent if we are to maintain moral and social order.  Someone once said that we are all in this huge boat together, and we owe each other a terrible loyalty.  This is true.  We especially owe our children a terrible loyalty.  We owe them some ethical, and moral instruction.  If such instruction does not occur in the home, it needs to be given somewhere, by someone, at sometime in the child's life.

With an eye then, toward healing the whole child, the solutions proposed in this chapter can be embraced by Christians, Buddhists, Hindus, Jews, members of all other religions, or atheists alike without compromising anyone's beliefs.

Currently, many schools are places where anything goes; where havoc and chaos are common; where there is a lack of regard for anyone else; where no one seems to be in charge; where discipline is undermined by dominant parents before fearful administrators; and where self is the only rule.  Isn't it time to find some common ground?  Because finding this common ground calls for sacrifices by everyone, however, we must first see the need.

## The Killing Fields Are Here

Teaching morals and values to children is imperative, because morals cannot be legislated and values cannot be judicially enforced. Neither can right behavior be coerced or policed.  Therefore, without some type of ethical law (which can only come from within us as a result of what we've learned about right and wrong) we shall all become savages.  One survivor of a concentration camp pleaded with the people of the world to help students to be human.  He saw gas chambers built by learned engineers; children tortured and poisoned by educated physicians; infants killed by trained nurses; and women and babies shot and burned by high school and college graduates. His request is that we help our students to become human so that we do not produce learned monsters, skilled psychopaths, or educated Eichmanns.

It is now time to apply the same self-searching honesty to this situation as we did to our underlying attitudes toward children in Chapter 7. We have a great need in our country for this honesty, which is crucial if we are to make the changes that are imperative.

When a teen-ager was arraigned for murder, his friends decried the high bail set by the judge saying, "What's the big deal, people die every day." Our need is great, our time is short, and we can no longer pretend that the rise in crime rates among children and the fall of education are not connected in part to the systematic elimination of all ethical, moral and values training within our country except within the confines of church property.

During 1996-1997, over 400,000 incidents of crime were reported in our nation's public schools. Since October 1997, eight violent shootings have occurred in eight months. Many have been killed. Many more have been wounded. The Killing Fields are upon us.


## The CatchAll First Amendment

If we are completely honest, and have nothing but the welfare of our children at heart, we know that the intent of the first amendment was not to abolish the religious values that were being taught in schools. Consider this: The same first Congress that gave us the First Amendment also gave us the Northwest Ordinance, which reads,

> "Religion, morality and knowledge being essential
> to good government, schools shall be established in
> the Northwest Territories."

Also, the Ordinance of 1787 calls for religious instruction in the land that would become Ohio. In fact, no nation on earth took greater pride in its moral heritage than did the United States.

Horace Mann also prescribed a system of education for the whole child.

> "In schools the principles of morality should be intermingled with the principles of science ... the multiplication tables should not have been more familiar, nor more frequently applied, than the rule, to do to others as we would that they should do to us."

It fell to later generations to remove all semblance of moral values or religion from our schools, and this removal has been consistently and successfully accomplished. This can be considered an education of sorts as well because in place of the previously taught values, we're training our children to believe that the First Amendment gives license to absolutely anything.

Children are not learning that the intent of the First Amendment was only to prevent the establishment of a national religion and to keep the national government from interfering with the religions of state and communities. Nor are they learning that free speech means Americans have the right to protest any form of tyranny or injustice such as they had experienced under English Rule. Instead, they are learning all the many interpretations of the amendment, most of which are skewed to fit the wants of the interpreters. What would our forefather writers of our constitution do if they knew how we have twisted that freedom to speak and publish into a license to make, advertise, and sell pornography, and then to pretend we do not see how easily available it is to our young?

The same founders of the Constitution also hired chaplains. Our senators are permitted to have the religious support, guidance, and prayer of chaplains, but our children are not. Go figure.

Not only has it become unpopular to have a conscience about spirituality, religion, or ethical, and moral behavior, we now go to great lengths to eradicate totally such topics from all learning. Even the Ten Commandments cannot be posted on some school walls (" ... lest the students reading these from day to day should be inclined to obey them") and prayer is denied the young people who ask for an invocation and benediction at their graduation exercises.

Some studies show that most Americans believe in God. Does this mean that the systematic eradication of all religious or moral values in schools is really the work and express rule of the minority? Well, that's a relief. Wouldn't it be horrible to find that the majority of Americans have brought us to our present condition willingly? Rather, we have brought ourselves to this condition (in part) by being afraid to step on the toes of certain groups or causes. There are surely more important things for us to fear. For example, in the absence of moral or ethical instruction, violence, pornography, crime, and drug use have flourished. In our heart of hearts, we know this is having an impact on our children's actions, at home, on the streets, and in schools.


**<u>Children Are Impressionable</u>**

> " 'Tis education forms the common mind:
>         Just as the twig is bent,
>             the tree's inclined."
>
> — Alexander Pope


We know children are impressionable. Just ordinary common sense tells us that we cannot constantly expose children to violent and pornographic images and not influence them. Try as we might to deny it, there is widespread proof of this influence; we're just not making the connection.

Try as we may to deny the "copycat syndrome," if we are completely honest with ourselves, we cannot. Cited here are only two of the many examples of this:

> "Shooting possibly inspired by movie. Dream
> scene shows classroom rampage. The 14-year-old
> boy charged with killing three classmates after a

prayer meeting told investigators he had seen it done in a movie, a prosecutor said Thursday.

"After Monday's shooting, investigators asked him had he ever seen this before, ever seen anything done like this, and he said, 'Yes, I have seen this done in Basketball Diaries.' "[1]

This is also true of pornography.

"Boys allegedly molested others viewing porn. The boys are accused of committing sexual acts with one 9-year-old and two 7-year-old boys. Two videos of commercially available X-rated movies can be linked to the activities ...."[2]

Can we honestly not make the connection?

There are those who claim that what children see (movies, television, concerts, videos, etc.) has no effect on them. One man told me that he himself had seen many movies where heroin was being shot and people were being blown away, and yet he had no desire to do any of these things. This must be denial. He's an adult. Does he honestly not understand that we are talking about impressionable children here, or impressionable troubled children who can be most adversely affected.

In addition, this is the day of rationalization. One such explanation came with this advertisement.

"Calvin Klein, what's he selling besides jeans? The ads features teen-age models in erotic poses .... The designer pulled the advertising campaign because he said the ads were 'Misunderstood by some.' He explained that the photographs intend to show that today's teens 'have a real strength of character and independence.' "[3]

This is another example of failure to connect.  He is using key words here that catch our attention and, by themselves, impress us. But strength of character is not built by showing children how to pose erotically and suggestively, and independence is not fostered by assuring the loss of children's innocence before their time.  That's the connection.  We must look beyond the words—even beyond the sentences.  We must look  beyond the moment to reach for meanings and to comprehend consequences.

> "Some people never learn anything, for this reason.  Because they understand everything too soon."
>
> — Pope


## And Who's Responsible?

Absolutely no one!  The prevailing attitude is:  "Whatever I did, I am not responsible.  There is someone in my background or in my life now that I can blame, if you'll just give me a moment or so to decide who that is.  But whoever, I am not responsible for my actions."  And our children are listening.

The prevailing attitude is entitlement.  "I have rights, and I am entitled to do what I please.  I don't care about whoever doesn't like it.  I don't care about who may be affected."  And our children are watching.

The prevailing religion is:  "If it feels good, do it.  If someone hurts you, hurt 'em back."  And our children are copying.

Hamilton County Juvenile Court Judge David Grossmann said in an interview:

> "These kids, as awful as many can be," he says, "are behaving in the world we adults have created for them.  They're mimicking the values they see rampant violence, demeaning behavior, incessant consumerism, 'my rights' above all else.

"We have sown the wind and we're reaping the whirlwind." The only permanent "fix," Grossmann believes, is for adults to reinstate some agreed-upon moral standards that favor the interests of children, families and communities.

"If we think we can protect and lead our children and do exactly as we please, we're living in fantasyland. Like it or not, adults, when making decisions, are going to have to ask, 'Is this going to be good for our kids—for mine and others?' "[4]

He's right. So, when innocent children are emotionally maimed and arrested in their learning, whom do we blame? Well, society either turns its face away or points an accusing finger at parents. The parents blame the teachers. Teachers blame the parents. And everyone blames society.

Actually everyone is responsible. When anyone rocks this big boat we're all in together, everyone is affected. Were we to neglect the physical care of our children as we've neglected their minds and their spirits, we would consider ourselves mad. Yet what we've done to the children of America is not merely a tragic failure for a few children, it is a profound loss for all humanity.

It is time to close the moral gap that exposes our children to violence, abuse, crime and pornography. Because no matter how you say it, explain it, rationalize it, disguise it, or package it, our children are vastly and adversely affected. Children are extremely impressionable. We need to make the connection between what adults do and what children become. And all of this predetermines what kind of learners our children will be.

"The supreme end of education is expert discernment in all things—the power to tell the good from the bad, the genuine from the counterfeit, and to prefer the good and the genuine to the bad and the counterfeit."

— Samuel Johnson

163

## It's a Three-Part System

"Education is the knowledge of how to use the whole of oneself."

— Henry Ward Beecher

Basically, the human system consists of three parts; and we must provide for all three because that is the way we were created. If you are religious, those three parts are the mind, the body, and the spirit. If you are not religious, the three parts are the mind, the body, and the heart, or whatever one wants to call our essential core of feeling. Whatever you believe concerning this, we all can agree that each part affects the other two, either happily or adversely.

Therefore, any learning that separates the head from the heart will ultimately be unsuccessful because if any one of the three parts of our system is neglected or not in good order, it will have an adverse effect on the contentment of the other two. They will not function well, if at all.

With our children, then, we must try to educate the mind, to develop the body, and to teach them to love and respect others. Inasmuch as right actions cannot be legislated, this can only come from within a person. This is the only place where children will learn about empathy and compassion and respect. Such emotions not only bring peace with one's neighbor, but also with one's self. Children who do not respect themselves cannot respect anyone else. Children who do not respect their teachers cannot learn from them. Children who do not respect their peers cannot learn with them.

Not only do children need to be loved by parents, teachers, and peers, they also need to love their parents, teachers and peers. Among the many other qualities of love is a firmness and discipline unequaled by anything else. Because when love recognizes something is undesirable or harmful to the welfare of the individual, it forbids such conduct.

The Japanese have a word that explains this—"kokkoro"— which means the general headquarters for heart and mind. They perceive it as one place and one state of being. Love is our humanizer. Everything that happens to us, everything we do works best if filtered through love.

Children must be encouraged to discover within themselves a sense of right and wrong, of true and false. The rising youth crime rates, the shootings in schools, and the fact that younger and younger children commit crimes have taught us that we can no longer leave the sole teaching of ethical behavior to parents.

We have been trying to educate our children by separating the heart from the head. This separates children from their emotions; it disciplines the child from the neck up. Children must be taught as a whole being—all three parts.

Victor Frankl, psychiatrist, author, and concentration camp survivor, had an understanding of human personality that differed from that of Sigmund Freud and other contemporaries. After his experience in the concentration camp, Frankl no longer agreed that the deepest drives in human nature were the will to pleasure and the will to power. His experiences led him to conclude that the most basic of all human drives is the will to meaning.

It's a three-part system. The mind may orchestrate power, and the body may be driven by pleasure, but it is the spirit or heart that must find "meaning" before one can be happy or fulfilled and therefore learn well. It's a three-part system, and we must attend to all three within our children because each single part so drastically affects the other two.

Louisa May Alcott said, "I am not afraid of storms, for I am learning how to sail my ship." When our children cannot read, cannot comprehend mathematics, and are spiritually or morally bereft, we are failing to provide them even with the means to struggle through life, much less to get through the storms.

*　　*　　*

If parents teach their children how to treat others with respect, so much the better. Reinforcement is good. If they do not (and many don't), shouldn't our children hear it somewhere, from someone, from some place, sometime in their lives? Our youth crime, drug, and illiteracy rates tell us that they should.

165

1) **<u>Bring children to an understanding of the word "neighbor."</u>**

The Killing Fields are here. When we fail to teach ethical behavior, we remove any kind of moral consciousness from within children. For the perpetuation of our society, we must find some way to live together in peace and order. For this to happen, children must be taught that the person sitting next to them has the same rights, hopes, fears, needs, feelings, and hurts that they do. We must teach our children about empathy.

2) **<u>All beliefs and religions must find common ground.</u>**

Actually, we already have, but we've either forgotten it or failed to make the connection. If you are a Christian, the Bible says, "Come now and let us reason together." If you do not recognize the deity of God, then, "Come now and let us reason together," said a wise man. We can take wisdom where we find it. For example, whereas I do not embrace his religion, Ghandi said many wise things. For example, he said that the thing that worried him the most was the hardness of the hearts of the educated. For the sake of all, then, let us take our wisdom from wherever it comes.

Reprinted with special permission of Nick Anderson and the Washington Post Writer's Group  5

The answer and the wisdom that would cure our schools, ourselves, our country and our social ills is this:

> "Therefore all things whatsoever ye would that
> others should do to you, do ye even so to them."

I know.  You've heard this before.  You certainly have.  Let us count the ways.

> "None of you is a believer until he loves
> for his brother what he loves for himself."
> — Mohammed

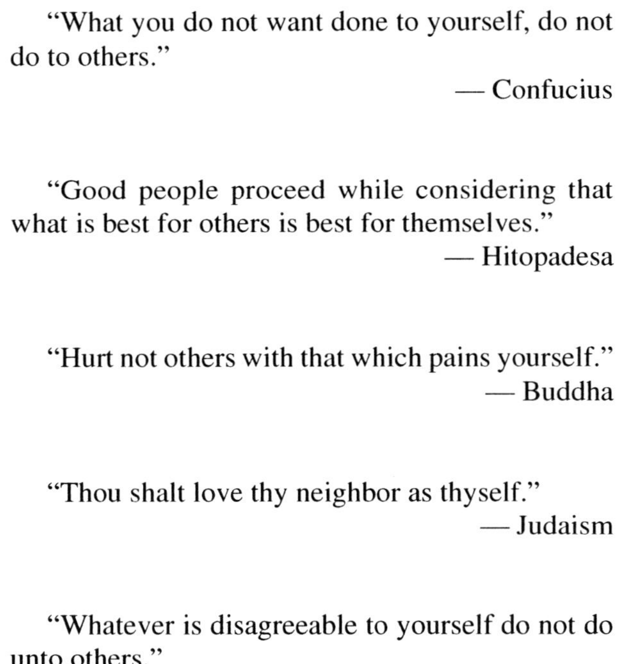

"What you do not want done to yourself, do not do to others."

— Confucius

"Good people proceed while considering that what is best for others is best for themselves."

— Hitopadesa

"Hurt not others with that which pains yourself."

— Buddha

"Thou shalt love thy neighbor as thyself."

— Judaism

"Whatever is disagreeable to yourself do not do unto others."

— Zoroastraianism

We may speak of great differences in religious beliefs and forms of worship around the world, but despite the fact that they are called by an endless number of names, they all expound the fundamental philosophy of the Golden Rule. Perhaps because the founders of all religions had the wisdom to realize that humankind cannot long exist without this philosophy being taught and practiced.

We're going to hear: "It's too simple and it won't work!" No, it's not simple, it's brief. Too often we confuse simplicity with brevity. A faith that rests on these tenets, that shook up an established religion of its day, that turned the first-century world upside down, and that rattled the teeth of a political system is not simple.[6] The Golden Rule is unequaled for assuring the preservation of a society.

And it does work.  Respecting self and others was the foundation for all discipline in my classrooms.  (You've hurt his person.  Would you like this same thing done to you?  Think about that.  Put yourself in this person's place.  Feel what he or she's feeling.  If you don't want the same thing done to you, then you don't do it to others.)  It works.  (The younger, the better, of course.)

Even four or five years later, when I saw my former students in the hall doing something wrong and they saw me, they stopped and lowered their eyes.  They remembered.  What if every other teacher had taught and reinforced this in every other grade?  What if this principle was incorporated into their course-work?  What if parents taught it?

Surely no cause or group can find fault with this teaching, because when this Rule is ignored, it comes back to bite us all.  Far too many are being killed because this Rule is not being taught.  Because it smacks of religion, many have diligently worked to remove it along with all ethical instruction from life as we know it.  I leave it to you to consider the totality of what obeying this rule could accomplish—from world wars to the classroom.


## 3) <u>Include the principles of the Golden Rule in coursework.</u>

Our reading curriculum should contain stories that build character and teach, not church doctrines, but morals, empathy, honesty, kindness, compassion, courage, perseverance, altruism, responsibility and fidelity to one's commitments and vows.  Even though they were fanciful, storybooks used to include these principles, and children loved them.

Somewhere along the way educators got the idea that children would be more interested in a repetition of what happens in their everyday lives.  Can we not have both?

For example, I wrote some of the poetry for the children's writing lessons.  They preferred writing these poems over writing dull boring sentences.  We would laugh at the story and discuss the moral it taught.  I would have them close their eyes and visualize the picture and then illustrate it after their other work was done.  "The Bird and The Bee" was one of their favorite poems.

A bird and a bee on a fence,
Were discussing their village defense,
    Said the bee, "Though a fighter
    I'm scared of a spider,
Their webs make me terribly tense!"

"Spiders bother me none," said the bird,
"To be scared of a web is absurd,
    I'm as brave as can be,
    Nothing ever scares me,
I suppose 'Hero's' probably the word."

Just then crept the cat 'round the tree,
So obviously hungry was she,
    With a shriek and a cry,
    The bird took to the sky,
"Goodbye, hero," laughed Mister Bee.


Moral

So never make fun of your brother,
Instead empathize with each other,
    For everyone here
    Has something they fear,
What scares one does not scare another.

— Norma Simpson


My intent is not, nor ever has been, to present church dogma to my schoolchildren, or to advance any one particular religious faith. My intent is to promote curricula that teaches needed lessons regarding "neighbor" in a pleasurable yet instructive manner. After eight violent school shootings in as many months, how desperately do we need this concept presented to our children?

When taught, the Golden Rule shows our children, through their reading and course material how to treat one another. It shows them that everyone else deserves the same respect they do, that freedom does not mean license, and that tolerance applies not only to race and religion, but also to late-blooming children who mature and learn at their own pace.

Also, let us not forget the connection between morals/virtues and responsibility.  Responsibility is a most important concept in all learning.


### 4) **<u>Children need to be taught manners.</u>**

In any society manners are essential to prevent chaos.  They are the traffic rules of the respect we owe all other human beings.


### 5) **<u>Adults must realize they are responsible.</u>**

All adults must look at what they want to do and then consider how that conflicts with the best interests of the children, who are surely watching.  Americans have seriously underestimated the perceptive abilities of children.  When I was still quite young, my father used to spell the word "show" when trying to find out if my mother wanted to go before he mentioned it to me.  (I wonder why?)  He would say to her, "Would you like to go to the s-h-o-w?"  I ended this little spelling game when I told them that I wanted to go to the "show-w" too.

Adults have also seriously underestimated how easily accessible X-rated movies, TV, videos, and phone services for ordering pornography are to children.  It is time to exercise self-discipline. The question should be, "Is this going to be good for our children, not only mine but others as well?"


### 6) **<u>Teach children WHY we behave well.</u>**

A most important concept for all teaching is to bring children to understand that we are good because it's the right thing to do.

Inasmuch as most of the problems afflicting society today are moral problems, they are remarkably resistant to government cures. Thus the people must depend on something other than the government to become civilized. The only way to further a civilized society is to instill virtue in our children.

We can't just tell children; we must help them understand it within themselves so as to foster all-important self-discipline. We cannot just coerce such behavior; the children must understand the concept. If they do not, they will behave only when someone is watching.


## 7)  <u>**Teach children about disabilities and ridicule.**</u>

Back to the Golden Rule. Children should be taught how it must feel to be blind, crippled, hearing-impaired, learning disabled, elderly, a late bloomer, etc. There is a school in England that teaches this. For example, a child will be blindfolded and required to live without being able to see for a time. What are the chances of this child ridiculing a person who is actually blind?


## 8)  <u>**Teach children the truth about consequences.**</u>

Children must learn that there are consequences to every action, and they must stand up and take responsibility for everything they do. They cannot blame anyone else for their actions.


## 9)  <u>**Teach children about immediate satisfactions.**</u>

Children must learn that an important part of their growth and development is to postpone certain immediate satisfactions for long-term goals. They cannot have everything they want, nor can they do everything they want to do—right now.

10) **<u>Revive the word "character."</u>**

> "Education has for its object the formation of
> character."
>
> — Herbert Spencer

Character, a concept that we have allowed to fall into disuse, has been replaced by the more popular term "personality." Whereas personality has more to do with emotions and behavioral tendencies, character is what persons of integrity exhibit. Let us not exclude the steady, more imperative character traits from the total self. As always, we need that vital balance.


11) **<u>Understand the difference between "instilling" and "policing."</u>**

American quality control expert W. Edwards Deming is credited with launching Japan's economic "miracle." Deming taught the Japanese how to design quality into products rather than to inspect it in. This is exactly what we must do with our children. We must start early and build within them the precepts of the Golden Rule and then teach them how to apply it. We must instill morality and virtue, rather than just trying to "police" them in. Policing virtue is merely a bandaid approach applied to older children because virtue was not taught when the children were moldable and more amenable to it.


12) **<u>Think more on our responsibilities than our rights.</u>**

"It's my right!" We hear this often. How often do we hear, "It's my responsibility?" It's time that we consider the state of our country and then, in the light of our findings, honestly reevaluate "rights" and "responsibilities."

# Chapter 9

The Children: The Real Teachers If We Would But Listen

"All truly wise thoughts have been thought already thousands of times, but to make them truly our own, we must think them over again honestly, until they take root in our personal experience."
— Johann Wolfgang Von Goethe

If you have read this book thoroughly from the heart, you can no longer be perplexed or lacking in knowledge concerning the situations confronting American children where they live and where they attempt to learn. It has presented you with the solutions for redesigning the school system and improving the lives of our children. For success, however, two things must happen.

First, whereas you may have thought the thoughts you've found in this book many times, to change the school system we must think them over again honestly enough to make them our own. Only when we make them enough a part of our own personal experience will we make the needed sacrifices to make the needed changes.

Secondly, all the solutions in this book must be implemented to bring about successful school reform. I've read books on children, books on administrators, books on money, books on readiness, etc. However, this author believes it is imperative for change and essential for results that all of these issues be brought together in one book so that we are working for reform from the perspective of a total picture. It's the only way to run a railroad.


## <u>The Key Element—Connection</u>

An old song that speaks of the head bone being connected to the neck bone, etc., illustrates why there is no "in part" solution. Just as the bones must be connected for the body to work properly, all the solutions in this book must be incorporated for the successful reform of the school system because they are bound in mutual dependency, each upon the other.

Children's success levels are connected to adult attitudes toward children, which are connected to the type of school systems adults will support. The type of school system is connected to the type of administrators and teachers the system allows. This in turn is connected to how the money is spent; which is connected to the morality of each adult in contact with children; which is connected to how much morality is instilled in children by teaching and example; which is connected to the children's happiness and success levels.

We have become a society so mired down in "our rights" that we have missed the connections. This is why our educational system is in such dire straits. Unfortunately, the damage from our lapses continues to broaden and spread. Although college costs keep escalating, what this money buys us is lessening. Required courses such as English, math and foreign languages have decreased and remedial courses have increased. Thus, we have come full circle from kindergarten to high school to college.

The answers have always been and will continue to be found within the children, who have been telling us for some time what they need. They've told us by their actions, their reactions, their tummyaches, their hurts and tears, their anxieties and hypersensitivities, their levels of self-esteem, their drug use, their crime and illiteracy rates and their anger and violent acts. Not only must we listen, we must take this knowledge to heart and make it our own—and then act upon it.

A review of all you've read so far makes it quite clear that the present educational system is not being run for children. Therefore, it is up to you, the readers, to storm the citadels of the school systems and to redesign them for the children. Good administrators with honest perplexities will welcome you. Others may fight to retain their power and to remain in control. For success, we must listen not to them, but to the children.

## Listen to the Children Regarding Grouping

We're not listening to children. Instead we listen to the arguments of the "experts." Some of those arguments are as follows: Mixing children exposes the 'academic whizzes' to other kinds of intelligence; mixing children promotes cooperation; mixing children boosts the quality of education for those less academically inclined, etc.

Yes, in mainstreaming " ...academic whizzes are exposed to other kinds of intelligence." So what exactly does this do for them? However profound this argument may sound on the surface, we are more likely to arrive at the truth by talking to young people who have actually experienced this approach. I have spoken with older students who came up through the mainstreaming system. During my interviews of sixth-, seventh-, and eighth-graders, I was amazed to learn what they know and understand about every area of the school system.  I was also amazed to find that in some school districts these older students are still not being grouped appropriately.  One seventh-grader said:

> "They're still putting us in classes with students who can't do what we do.  I'm in this reading group where many of them read so slowly that I get really bored, so I'll read on ahead.
>
> "But as sure as I do that, the teacher will ask me where we are.  I don't know, and so I get in trouble. So then I try to stay with the one reading, but they read so slowly that by the time they're finished, I've lost the meaning of the story.
>
> "The one who is reading is stammering and struggling over every word, so I can't tell what's going on.  So it's read ahead, know what I've read and be punished; or follow along and not know what I've read so I can't answer questions and have the teacher think I'm stupid.  Either way I'm in trouble. I can't win."

This is what not grouping properly does to academic whizzes. What it does for children of lesser ability or for the unready was covered earlier in Chapter One.

"It promotes cooperation."  Most often what it promotes is resentment and ridicule and embarrassment.  Seldom does one feel like cooperating with those they resent and envy or with those who are either laughing or feeling sorry for them.

"It boosts the quality of education for those less academically inclined."  Mostly it boosts a feeling of failure as the child suffers under the "they can do it, I can't, what's wrong with me" syndrome.

## **Listen to Children Regarding Learning Methods**

There are two kinds of learning: Extrinsic and Intrinsic. Extrinsic learning involves a mechanical approach. It is achieved from the outside—the teacher is active and the child is passive. This kind of learning has little or nothing to do with the unique qualities of the learning.

Children accumulate what they are given. Whether they lose or retain it depends on the efficiency of the indoctrination process and on each child's responsiveness. This type of learning reflects the goals of the teacher and largely ignores the values, goals, and needs of the learner.

This extrinsic learning is characteristic of approximately 90 percent of the kind of teaching to which most children are subjected—i.e., learning associated with drill, repetition, and memorization of facts. The teacher is the lecturer, conditioner, and reinforcer. The children are receptors who are force-fed information that, hopefully, they can then spit out on a test at the end of the week.

Intrinsic learning is partially unconscious in nature. It includes those experiences during which we learn who we are, what we love, and what we value. With this type learning, the teacher is a prompter, guide, helper, and counselor. Galileo spoke to this when he said:

> "You cannot teach a man anything. You can only
> help him discover it within himself."

With intrinsic learning, children are alive and active in the learning setting rather than just being spectators. Also, this type of learning has rhythms, which include unproductive and then productive times. In the current school system, no room is allowed for this natural rhythm in learning. Instead, it is assumed that each morning a child will be able to put out the standard quota of learning effort required to progress at a standard rate through a standard curriculum at a standard level.

Children need both types of learning. They are telling us what they need through their test scores, illiteracy rates, and reactions.

In large classrooms, containing children of all different ability levels, however, intrinsic learning is more difficult ( if not impossible) to implement.


## <u>Listen to Children Regarding Testing</u>

Parents depend on test scores and grades to determine their children's progress.  Therefore, many things must be considered before accepting the veracity of test scores.

One State Board member told me that the test scores reported in the newspapers are correct.  When I asked how scores could be so horrible one year and show improvement the next in an unchanged system,  she explained how test questions are revised every seven years in her state.  By the end of a seven-year period, the teachers know how to teach to them.  So the scores begin to improve in the latter years of the cycle.  In this then, we see that children are not really improving, they are just learning how to answer certain questions.  The scores will drop when there's a new set of questions.

There are, therefore, many questions to ask regarding test scores.  Are the test questions and answers being taught to the children by teachers before the testing?  Are the scores being reported accurately?  Are they being reported honestly?  Are they inflated for poorer students?  Are they averaged, clustered, arranged, or separated so we look good when compared with other nations?  Are they using the same tests year after year?  How much do tests show when they are just facts the children are taught to memorize beforehand so they can duplicate them on the tests?   If any of the preceding affect scores, then the results are distorted and parents do not really know how well their children are learning.

In some states, this teaching to the tests is done quietly, with no one admitting that it happens.  On a recent trip to another state, however, I was surprised to find this teaching to the test is done quite openly.  In fact, some sixth- and seventh-graders told me they were actually given booklets containing the exact questions and answers that the tests would contain.  When I appeared somewhat skeptical, they produced the booklets (which I now have in hand). One sixth-grader said:

> They give us this booklet and we're supposed to learn all the facts in it. Some parents are actually called and told to give their children 'brain food' on the morning of the tests.

> "But when we get to school, they give us orange juice and donuts, just in case. On the morning of the testing I was sick, and when I didn't show up at school, my teacher called my parents and told them I had to come to take the tests. I'm an "A" student, so she insisted that I be there.

> "If we don't do well on the tests, we are punished. Like recess is taken away or we can't talk at lunch."

When I asked this girl why she thought this was taking place she said, "Because our school gets money according to how well we do on our tests."

Concerning what the tests really tell us about our children's learning skills, we should remember this: If children are merely putting down answers they've memorized how valid are these scores? More important, is this true learning?

## <u>Odds and Ends</u>

<u>Other solutions.</u>   In desperation we have come up with other solutions to improve education. Some have been most detrimental; others pose serious questions.

For example, the Voucher System proponents must answer some questions for us; such as, can every child in a city go to the best schools in that city? Will there be room in the better schools for every child who wants to attend? If not, who has to sit in the bad schools? How do children in poorer neighborhoods get to these better schools many miles removed from their homes?  What will this cost?  Will every child be admitted to the school of their choice or can these better schools pick and choose children?  Will this encourage "elitism"?  Will mainstreaming still be the system of choice?  Will phonics be taught?

The Voucher System is supported in some measure because the public system is so bad and the situation seems so hopeless.  I understand this.  The situation is not hopeless, however, and the better way is to fix the public school system for every child.


<u>Computers.</u>  Computers may be a good teaching tool if care is taken to use them appropriately, especially in early grades.  For example, more teachers and smaller classes must be a first priority if computers are an option—not larger classes and fewer teachers so as to afford computers.  This happens in some districts where administrators believe they are "the answer."

Also, computers should be an "addition"—not an "in-place-of"—to a curriculum that allows time for intrinsic learning—that learning which challenges children to think, ponder, and reason, and to memorize poems and readings (a lost art).  In one district my supervisor required my first-graders to spend too much time on the computer which took such valuable time from reading instruction.  No school district can afford to do this.


<u>The Ratings Game</u>.  The debate rages on over the academic superiority of private schools versus public schools. Academically, however, this is not always measurable.  Public schools are unique in that they cannot turn a child away for any reason.  On the other hand, private schools can be most selective.  For example, if a private school has a child who is a severe discipline problem, they can transfer this child to the public school.  (Actually in some families, a troubled child will go to the public school, while his siblings continue to attend the private school.)

Also, when private schools do not have remedial reading or learning disability classes, they can also transfer these children to public schools.  To take nothing away from either system, this is the way it is, and it's okay.  Only thing is, there are too many variables to make any accurate academic comparison between the two situations.


## <u>Elements To Consider When Focusing on the Child</u>

As a nation we must focus on and revive "childhood" and allow children to be children. That carefree, joyful time can easily be lost. Adults have fallen into a fast-forward mode that believes it better for children to be rushed into being adults. Children need to know that it's okay to be imaginative, to laugh, and to pretend. They need to know that they have the time—to just be children. We must allow childhood its full measure.

Another element to consider is that, if not pushed and stressed, children will exhibit signs and evidence of their interests, gifts, and talents. These help us to discover exactly what they need from us.

Children will become exactly what we bring out in them or what we develop, encourage, foster, coax, or provoke to emerge. Like a diamond, they contain thousands of facets and possibilities within. As with a diamond, the more sides that are cut and developed, the greater the brillance. To consider the wonder and mystery of human possibility, to enhance the specialness of each child, and to elicit the unique potential that is already hidden present some awesome responsibilities for each adult. Awesome, yes, but also challenging and rewarding.

Young children are so dear, trusting, loving and malleable. This malleability disappears with age, however,
and time is of the essence when attempting to develop all the possibilities that lie within them.

Time is an essential concept in both raising and in teaching children who know their importance by how much time we give them. Children need time with adults so they can express their hopes, dreams, feelings, fears, problems, and love; adults must give them this time.

If our children are grouped properly, teachers will no longer have to divide their time in so many different ways. Instead, all this valuable time can be focused in their small classes on children who are all at the same place. Children know their importance by the amount of time we give them.

Children have feelings. This is another critical truth regarding children that has (in some measure) been forgotten. They feel and they hurt. Mainstreaming was instituted by those who forgot that children have feelings and are easily embarrassed. Many parents also have forgotten that children have feelings and can be emotionally scarred by abusive actions and language. Some teachers, too, have forgotten that children have feelings and can be embarrassed and traumatized before their peers. And all of them have forgotten how these feelings can affect learning.

As previously stated in Chapter 2, school is where the five- and six-year-old first begins to see themselves as a member of a group. This group, however, subdivides into the "in" group and the "out" group. The children in the "out" group experience all the pain and all the trauma that rejection can heap upon them.

Colorado sociologists Peter and Patti Adler researched student popularity and spoke to these "in" and "out" groups. Their findings were reported in part as follows:

> "Out means you'll be teased after school, you'll hear threats, there will be fights or intense teasing on the bus.
>
> "To adults 'teasing' may sound innocuous. To kids who live with it every day—who spend Sunday nights dreading it—can be stomach-turning torment."[1]

This is happening, not just to older children, but to five- and six-year-olds as well. We need to change the system.

<u>**To Sum Up**</u>

> "In leading a child, you may be commanding an
> army.
> — Horace

If America's children are to become literate, compassionate, empathetic, happy, productive members of the society that they themselves must preserve and perpetuate, we must return to the time when learning was successful. We must return to the time when it was known that all adults bear some responsibility for what our children become; when we understood that the fate of our nation depends on the education of our young.

> "Next in importance to freedom and justice is
> popular education, without which neither freedom
> or justice can be permanently maintained.
> — James A. Garfield

My intent throughout this book has been either to introduce or to remind a nation of the elegant truths regarding our children that have been so inelegantly disregarded. Some of these truths are:

- Our children need to be physically, mentally, and emotionally ready for each task before they are expected to perform it.

- They need to be able to decode all the new words they encounter their whole life long (phonics).

- Children need good teachers who are allowed to be creative, caring, and focused rather than teachers who are mandated into immobility.

- They need to work from success rather than from frustration, boredom, or mortification.

- They need smaller classes, therefore they need a larger percentage of the education dollars to be funneled to the classroom.

- Children need instruction on how to love and respect their neighbor.

- They need adults to respect them as persons and to understand their vulnerability.

- Most imperatively children need to be taught empathy, compassion, and how to put themselves in another's place.

- Children need to believe in themselves.

- They need a firmness and constancy in disciplinary matters from parents, teachers, and administrators who uphold the rules from a "tough love" stance in a united front.

- They need for adults to listen to them.

- Children need to be allowed the time to be children rather than miniature adults.

Americans must not only "hold these truths to be self-evident," but they must hold them as timeless, and understand that we ignore them to our peril.  Our nation's present condition shows us that to a large extent we have ignored them.

In the light of all these truths, then, let us place our children's needs first, before adult wants.  It's time.

*　　　*　　　*

French philosopher John Paul Sartre believed that we invent ourselves by virtue of the multitude of our choices.  This author believes that for the most part—beyond biological factors—children are the sum total of adult choices. What adults live and place before children can decide their morality and their character. How adults treat children in the home can decide their mental well-being and emotional stability,.

AND, what adults decide regarding education makes our children either readers, or illiterate (or nearly illiterate) members of a society in which they cannot operate beyond mere existence.


## **One Last Thought**

"When the well's dry, we know the worth of the water."

— Benjamin Franklin


In our nation, we are beginning to see the worth of the objectives of education that have been lost to us. We must recapture those lost objectives. From the present condition of our educational system, we must admit that we have been blind to those objectives because we have focused too often on the causes we support, the rights we espouse, the political correctness we defend, and the party loyalty we embrace. What I am asking, for the children's sake, is to put all these things second to the objective that our children learn to read.

Refuse to allow any of these things, or anything else, to determine that a child must sit in a situation where he or she can never succeed or even learn to read. There will be time enough afterward to fight your battles and promote your causes. The question is simply this—what will these rights or causes mean to the children if they must face the future unable to read?

Let us redesign the school system for the sake of every child.

# Epilogue

An elderly gentleman rushed into the office one evening to tell me a most important thing. He said that he'd had a dream about me and the first thing he wanted me to understand was that he normally dreamed in black and white, but this dream was in color.

Never having considered dreams or their meanings in great depth, I started to speak but he rushed on enthusiastically.

"I saw you sitting at a table that was high on a hill. Stacks and stacks of your book were on the table. And then, winding over hills and valleys for as far as the eye could see I saw a single line of thousands and thousands of . . . "

Yes, I knew, the parents, of course. He was still speaking.

" ....their arms were held out, reaching for the book."

"Yes," I said, "the parents."

He became even more emphatic. "NO! No, not parents—children. The line was made up of children, with their arms out, reaching ...."

Whatever we may believe about dreams, this one spoke in truth. Whereas parents and citizens must read and process the information, it truly is the children who wait and "reach out" for change. It is the children who wait on a school system that has been designed just for them.

# Appendix

## Introduction

1. Sydney J. Harris, Reprinted with special permission of North America Syndicate, King Features Syndicate, A Unit of the Hearst Corporation.

## Chapter 1

1. Reprinted by special permission of the Associated Press, The Cincinnati Post, September 30, 1991, p. 1.
2. The National Commission on Excellence in Education/U.S., Dept. of Ed., A Nation at Risk, April 1983, p. 5.
3. Ibid., p. 8.
4. National Education Goals Panel, The National Education Goals Report: Building a Nation of Learners, Washington, DC: U.S. Government Printing Office, 1997, pp.8-9.
5. Loc. Cit., A Nation at Risk.
6. Educational Testing Service, U.S. Department of Education, Adult Literacy in America, September 1993, p. XV.
7. The National Education Goals Panel, U.S. Department of Education, The National Education Goals Report, Building a Nation of Learners, 1995, p.12.
8. Reprinted by permission of Dr. Joseph S. Renzulli, Professor, Educational Psychology, University of Connecticut, The National Research Center on The Gifted and Talented.
9. Op. Cit., A Nation at Risk, p. 11.
10. From SUMMERHILL:FOR AND AGAINST, Copyright c. 1970. Passage from section written by Eda LeShan. Originally published by Hart Publishing Company, Inc.

## Chapter 2

1. "Stress and Your Child," Dr. Archibald D. Hart, c. 1992, Word Publishing, Nashville, Tennessee. All rights reserved, p. 7.
2. From "THE CONSPIRACY AGAINST CHILDHOOD," by Eda J. LeShan. Copyright 1967 by Eda LeShan. Originally published by Atheneum Books, p.6.
3. Why Johnny Can't Read by Rudolf Flesch. Copyright 1955 by Harper & Brothers, renewed by Rudolf Flesch, p. 11.
4. Printed by special permission of Dr. Robert Gregory, Pediatrician, Cincinnati, Ohio.

## Chapter 3

1. Sidney J. Harris, Reprinted with special permission of North America Syndicate.
2. The Cincinnati Enquirer, From the Editorial Page, opinions from Opinion Page, Reprinted by permission of Peter Bronson, Editorial Page Editor, Thursday, January 16, 1997,p. A16.
3. By permission of Mike Luckovich, and Creators Syndicate. The Atlanta Constitution, Atlanta Georgia, March 1, 1992.
4. Permission granted by the Investor's Business Daily, Where Are Edu-fads hatched? By Ben Boychuk, Wednesday, October 15, 1997.
5. Printed by special permission of Dr. Jeanne S. Chall, Professor of Education and former Director of the Reading Laboratory at the Graduate School of Education, Harvard University.
6. Reprinted with permission of Investor's Business Daily, article by Ben Boychuk, Wednesday, October 15, 1997.

## Chapter 4

1. Sydney J. Harris, Reprinted with special permission of North America Syndicate, King Features Syndicate, A Unit of the Hearst Corporation.

2. Printed with permission by the Reverend Tom Conley, Vicar, The Episcopal Church of the Annunciation, Marietta, Georgia, Sermon.

**Chapter 6**

1. The Cincinnati Enquirer, "Property Taxes up 89% in Decade," Wednesday, April 3, 1996.
2. The Cincinnati Enquirer, "Sick Days Become Retirement Bonanza," Sunday, February 15, 1998, p. 1.
3. The Cincinnati Enquirer, From the Editorial Page, opinions from Opinion Page, Reprinted by permission of Peter Bronson, Editorial Page Editor, Thursday, January 16, 1997.
4. Reprinted with special permission of King Features Syndicate, Editorial Cartoon, by Jim Borgman.
5. Reprinted with special permission of King Features Syndicate, Editorial Cartoon, by Jim Borgman.
6. From Thieves of innocence. This material is copyrighted and permission to use information has been granted by the Ankerberg Theological Research Institute, p. 7.

**Chapter 7**

1. Sydney J. Harris, Reprinted with special permission of North America Syndicate, King Features Syndicate, A Unit of the Hearst Corporation.
2. The Cincinnati Enquirer, permission granted by Enquirer News Wires and Staff Reports, February 11, 1993.
3. Cartoon, Marshall Clark, The Cincinnati Enquirer, 1993, Reprinted with permission of Marshall Clark.
4. Sydney J. Harris, Reprinted with special permission of North America Syndicate, King Features Syndicate, A Unit of the Hearst Corporation.

## Chapter 8

1.  From the Associated Press, Permission granted by William E. Ahearn, Vice President, Executive Editor, Friday, December 5, 1997.
2.  The Cincinnati Enquirer, Friday, February 19, 1993.
3.  The Cincinnati Enquirer, From the Editorial Page, opinions from Opinion Page, Permission granted by Peter Bronson, Editorial Page Editor, August 31,1995.
4.  The Cincinnati Enquirer, From the Editorial Page, opinions from Opinion Page, Permission granted by Peter Bronson, Editorial Page Editor, Wednesday, August 9, 1995, p. A8.
5.  Editorial Cartoon, by Nick Anderson, The (Louisville) Courier-Journal, Reprinted by permision of The Washington Post Writers Group.
6.  Printed with permission by the Reverend Tom Conley, Vicar, The Episcopal Church of the Annunciation, Marietta, Georgia, Sermon.

## Chapter 9

1.  The Cincinnati Enquirer, Monday, March 8, 1993.